Hidden selves

Hidden selves

An exploration of multiple personality

Edited by

*Moira Walker and
Jenifer Antony-Black*

Open University Press
Buckingham · Philadelphia

Open University Press
Celtic Court
22 Ballmoor
Buckingham
MK18 1XW

email: enquiries@openup.co.uk
world wide web: http://www.openup.co.uk

and
325 Chestnut Street
Philadelphia, PA 19106, USA

First Published 1999

ISBN 0 335 20200 4 (pb) 0 335 20201 2 (hb)

A catalogue record of this book is available from the British Library

Library of Congress Cataloging-in-Publication Data
Hidden selves: an exploration of multiple personality / Moira Walker and Jenifer Antony-Black, eds.
      p.   cm.
   Includes bibliographical references and index.
   ISBN   0-335-20201-2 (hardcover). – ISBN   0-335-20200-4 (pbk.)
   1. Multiple personality. 2. Multiple personality–Case studies.
I. Walker, Moira. 1948– . II. Antony-Black, Jenifer, 1947–
RC569.5.M8H53 1999
616.85'236–dc21
                                                                   99–17602
                                                                       CIP

Copy-edited and typeset by The Running Head Limited, www.therunninghead.com
Printed in Great Britain by Biddles Limited, Guildford and King's Lynn

To all the women who have survived abuse.
They are not victims: in their own way each is a survivor.

Contents

Acknowledgements

A special thankyou to Liza and her different selves for agreeing to share their experiences with the editors and the authors and all the readers of this book. We would like to thank all the women we have worked with over the years who have taught us so much. We would also like to thank all those who have helped us in our own training and development, and our friends who have given us so much support.

Chapter 1

A century of controversy: multiplicity or madness; memory or make believe?

Moira Walker

Introduction

This book aims to further the discussion on multiple personality, a subject that is the focus of both serious therapeutic enquiry and rather more dramatic media attention. The seven contributing authors are all practitioners who have experience in working with adult survivors of abuse and who also have an interest in multiple personality. As readers will see, their individual views encompass a wide range of attitudes, beliefs and responses. In this book the common and shared strand is that they all discuss these within the context of the story of one survivor of abuse – Liza.

The authors come from a variety of theoretical backgrounds, but this may not be directly relevant or related to their individual responses: sharing a theoretical base does not imply unanimity of views with regard to multiple personality. As abuse itself is not limited to, or predicted by, class, race or gender, responses to multiple personality cannot be simply predicted by theoretical persuasion alone. As will be demonstrated throughout this book, opinions are divided and questions abound. Some people question whether multiple personality even exists, while others are clear that it does, stressing the need to understand its causation and explore appropriate therapeutic responses. Sceptics argue that multiple personality is the invention of over-zealous therapists, or a product of modern times, or a dramatic but essentially false presentation of self; while those who challenge this view see it as a complex defence: a psychological survival mechanism, usually a response to extreme childhood abuse.

In the next chapter readers will be introduced to Liza's story, told in her own words. Many hours were spent with Liza as she took the time she needed to describe her life as a child and as a adult. Throughout the process of bringing together this book Liza has had ongoing support and this will continue as long as is necessary. Her story is a deeply moving one and we are very grateful to her for taking the time and having the courage to allow us to use it. Liza became known to us via a colleague who knew that we were interested in producing a book on multiple personality and that we hoped to base the discussion on the life history of a real person. She knew that Liza was at a point in her life where she felt able to tell her story and for it to be the basis for further discussion. When you have read her story you might take some time to consider your own responses – how you would understand this material and the questions that arise for you – before reading the responses of the authors. It is hoped that the range of views, definitions, and responses to multiple personality will then provide readers with further opportunities to question, think and challenge for themselves.

As for many other survivors there can be a very positive side to speaking and being heard: both privately, as in therapy, or more publicly – albeit anonymously – in a book. In the latter instance there can be a powerful sense of something positive having come from a dreadful experience: there is a hope and an expectation that others will learn from it. Conversations with Liza were taped and my job was to transcribe the tapes and to put the material into chapter form. Some detail has been changed but only where necessary to protect Liza's anonymity. We wanted to ground this book in the life story of a real person, recognizing that it is a controversial subject. We felt it was crucial continually to remind ourselves and readers that at the centre of this are actual people. There is always a danger that controversy (particularly where anything related to abuse is concerned) may take on a life and purpose of its own and survivors be overlooked. They become caught up in an unhelpful web of argument and counter-argument. Just like the abused child they can too easily be again rendered invisible, insignificant and inaudible. Hence our concern to keep one person's story clearly in the spotlight.

In this chapter I am going to describe my own background and the interests that I bring to this book, and provide an overview of both the history of multiple personality and the current debates. I will also explore and discuss some questions relating to memory and its recovery. As I will show, the latter has become intertwined with, and linked to, all explorations of multiple personality. The 'recovered memory' debate spotlights the question of how traumatic experiences are dealt with by the child victim and adult survivor in terms of amnesia, the splitting off of traumatic experiences and later memory return. This is particularly pertinent as those with multiplicity describe how different personalities hold different memories. As will be seen in Liza's account the recovery of memories is mentioned almost immediately.

My own interest in abuse and in multiple personality

My co-editor, Jenifer Antony-Black, explains in her own chapter her history as it relates to her current work with abuse survivors, including those with multiple personality. As readers will see this is a subject of considerable personal and professional interest to her. My own interest in working with abuse survivors and my interest in multiple personality are also long lived. I have come to the latter by accident rather than intention. As with most practitioners it presented itself to me: I did not seek it out. I started my career as a young and untrained child care officer. I went on to train in social work, and worked with children, families and in mental health before training in psychotherapy. In my earliest days of working with children I was forced to recognize the horrors perpetrated on children; I remember when I was in my early twenties the shock of having to face that parents could batter their baby so severely that she was blinded and deafened. My ability to deny was challenged early, and on numerous occasions throughout my career I have had to believe through dint of hard evidence what I would have preferred to think of as simply unbelievable. I also began to realize that a refusal to recognize something as a possibility could mean that I would not see or hear and might even not be told.

Believing that abuse did happen seemed more straightforward for me than it was for some others. I have always held a sense of the world and people in it as being capable of both appalling acts of unspeakable cruelty and of true humanity, courage and care. After my first experience of being faced with abuse it has never surprised me, although it has horrified me. Having been introduced early to the horrors of physical abuse, recognizing the equally harsh realities of sexual abuse was another step. On reflection I think I was naively surprised by the resistance of so many to it and the aggression with which they could express this resistance. I was also forced to face that a powerful theme, where abuse is concerned, is the need and desire of so many to deny. Abuse is an uncomfortable truth. As we now know, much abuse occurs within the family, and this challenges the myth of the happy and supportive family as universally the best place to bring up our children: clearly for many children their reality is in direct contradiction with this myth.

However, if that myth is seriously challenged this will have huge resource and social policy implications. The question has to be asked: if the incest taboo is broken so frequently then is it really a taboo? If incest is not a taboo then the implications are deeply alarming. Successive governments may not be good at defining what the family is, but they have in common holding this concept close to the heart of their policies. Perpetrators have an obvious vested interest in denying abuse. Not all perpetrators act solely as individuals: large and complex organizations and rings exist. They very carefully cover their tracks, and nowadays are greatly assisted in both their operation and in their sophisticated systems of denial by advances in technology. Others also want to deny: the relatives of abuse survivors and others who may have known, or could have known, as well as all those who did not intervene and who could have done, including significant numbers employed as professional carers. And in general it is not comfortable to know about such nastiness – it challenges the illusion that the world is sufficiently safe and benign. Additionally, in today's age, when we are bombarded with media images of war and suffering, there may be a paradox at work: the more people are exposed to obvious and extreme suffering the less they are able to absorb it as real. In 1998 the extensive and moving Remembrance Day tributes to the veterans and the deceased in the First World War were perhaps only possible because for most people it is now sufficiently far away to make it safe to acknowledge the appalling and unnecessary pain and suffering of that war.

It is not surprising, then, that those who work with abuse survivors are used to working in a controversial field. Those like myself who have worked with abuse survivors for some years have gone through the gamut of working amid conflict and disagreement. There have been attacks, particularly on social workers, for either acting too precipitously and removing children from the bosom of happy families, or, conversely, for uncaringly leaving children to suffer further assault and not being sufficiently decisive. Therapists have been accused of not believing in the reality of abuse; then they are attacked for persuading clients that they have been abused and for planting false memories. In the midst of this they continue to try to work to help very unhappy clients, having themselves to cope with and survive hearing daily about the horrors perpetrated on children, and witnessing the sometimes devastating effects on adults.

While most workers are not actively involved in the controversies over issues such as memory and multiple personality they are inevitably affected by them, and quite often left feeling demoralized and undermined. Generally, whether in the voluntary sector, the National Health Service or the social services, they are over-worked, coping with long waiting lists, and are valiantly trying to respond as effectively as possible within the shortest possible time to unhappy and distressed clients. They are not on the look-out for either abuse or manifestations of multiple personality and they are too busy to get involved with spurious debate. In my experience of working in these settings, and in supervising and training others who work in them, workers are generally quietly trying to manage; they are not seeking extra work. Indeed, they are often rather desperately trying to cope with what is there already.

Over the years many of us have had to accept some awful realities of physical abuse and sexual abuse: that this affects large numbers of children and adults (and I suspect that we will never have a truly accurate picture of how many); that women can sexually abuse or be actively involved; that boys are as vulnerable as girls; that abuse is not the occasional aberration of a disturbed and dysfunctional individual but can be a highly organized business involving large numbers of men and women through many generations; that individual perpetrators can be extraordinarily organized and abuse huge numbers of carefully targeted children over many years; that the most vulnerable of children and adults can be greatly at risk (for example, those with learning difficulties); that abuse is widespread within our care institutions; that those deemed as carers can also be perpetrators and work hard in order to put themselves in those very positions. The list is endless and those of us who work in the field often wonder what we will have to face next. We have also had to recognize that the effects of abuse are complex, that at any point in time there is much we cannot comprehend and that our knowledge is always incomplete. We learn to be cautious and we recognize that previous certainties have crumbled into mythology.

My own interest in multiple personality has grown slowly over time. I became increasingly aware clinically of the ability of survivors of abuse to dissociate. In listening to them recalling childhood abuse (remembering that many survivors come for help with clear recall of what has happened to them, particularly when abuse was in mid or later childhood or in adolescence) it was evident that for many the ability to remove themselves from their body, to look down upon themselves, to enter an object in the room, and to cut off from feeling any pain, were very real unconscious strategies for survival. This was no great surprise to me and often reminded me of how people describe their experiences following other traumas such as accidents. These descriptions of dissociative episodes were not invited by me; they were told very hesitantly by the client. In my clinical work I have noted that survivors have a marked hesitancy in describing their experiences, especially where these have a bizarre or unusual quality. In the same way details of the abuse, even when clearly recalled, are often shared only with the greatest difficulty and sometimes not at all. Given that so many abused children have been threatened into silence or not been believed when they have told, and have lived in crazily contradictory worlds, such hesitancy is hardly surprising. In my work with such clients I always take great care never to make suggestions as to the source of their difficulties, and I believe that this carefulness is typical of any competent therapist. I would never use the word abuse unless it is first used by the client, and similarly I would never jump in precipitously with a label – including multiple personality. However, I also attempt never to deny the valid experience of a client, or to collude with the denial of others, and it is this balance that I try to achieve.

As far as I know I have worked with an extremely small number of clients whose level of dissociation and splitting has seemed to me to constitute multiple personality, although I have worked with very large numbers of clients who have childhood abuse in their history. I am aware, in saying this, that we once thought only a very few people had experienced sexual abuse. I remain clear that my knowledge is incomplete and I hold an open mind. However, I do introduce this book from the perspective that multiple personality (or 'dissociative identity disorder' as it is now more often referred to) is a presentation that I believe exists; that it is at a most extreme point on the continuum of dissociation and splitting; and that in my experience it is caused by extreme, repeated and often sustained attacks on a child over a period of years, attacks that are experienced as life threatening by that child. This is likely to be in a context where at least one of the perpetrators (and there may be many) is the person the child most closely depends upon; in a situation where there is no possibility of literal escape, only psychological escape; where the child has been forced not to tell and in a situation in which reality and non-reality are often strangely merged. I am also aware than any term, any presentation, any label is open to misuse, over-use, misinterpretation and unhelpful dramatization. But inappropriate usage does not render the concept itself irrelevant or void of meaning. Although my experience would lead me to feel that this extreme form of dissociation is relatively rare, other writers and practitioners in this book and elsewhere may disagree; and in writing these words I am aware of previously having made suppositions in this field that time has shown to be inaccurate.

The theoretical background to multiple personality

Other authors in this book refer to theoretical aspects pertinent to their own perspectives, and what follows here is aimed at providing a theoretical overview that augments what is written elsewhere. The concept of multiple personality is not new, although interest in it has waxed and waned over the last century. This is somewhat in parallel to the process in relation to abuse more generally: abuse has been well documented for the last hundred years, but response to this has been marked by pendulum swings of acknowledgement followed by denial. Pierre Janet was the first to formulate a theory of multiple personality in his discussion (1889) of 'successive existences'. He argued that the origin of this splitting arose from past traumatic events. Similar views were expressed by William James (1890) and Morton Prince (1906, 1914, 1919). Freud was familiar with the work of Janet, and some of Freud and Breuer's formulations in *Studies on Hysteria* (1895) were at that stage quite close to those of Janet. Debates in these early years focused on the causes of splitting rather than on its occurrence and significance, but this was to change; and Freud went on to develop a different model of the mind, in which the concept of repression took a central place. Repression was described as a 'horizontal split' between conscious and unconscious, quite at odds with the 'vertical split' between separate aspects of consciousness discussed by Janet, Prince and Breuer.

In this way Janet's concept of dissociation and its links with multiple personality was overtaken by Freud's concept of repression – one of his four cornerstones of psychoanalysis. Also, the centrality of the Oedipus complex in Freud's thinking with its accompanying emphasis on the sexual fantasies of children, which so profoundly influenced psychoanalytic thinking, emphasized the power of internal processes and conflicts rather than actual external assault. This has undoubtedly led to many who have been abused not being heard, and to the symptoms of their distress being wrongly interpreted and treated. Ferenczi expressed a different and challenging viewpoint, and in his famous and controversial paper written and presented in 1932 (although unpublished until 1955), he examines the effects of childhood sexual trauma on his patients. He argues that ongoing assault on the child creates fragmentation and splits within the child:

> If the shocks increase in number during the development of the child, the number and the various kinds of splits in the personality increase too, and soon it becomes extremely difficult to maintain contact without confusion with all the fragments each of which behaves as a separate personality yet does not know of even the existence of the others, fragmentation one would be justified in calling atomization.
>
> (Ferenczi 1955: 165)

It is interesting to note that his paper, read at the International Psycho-Analytic Congress in 1932, provoked a storm of criticism leading to his exclusion from psychoanalytic circles. The attack on him was extraordinary – to the extent that the rumour was spread that a nervous breakdown was responsible for these ideas. Abuse has always had the ability to trigger extreme responses.

Klein also linked splits within the personality as arising from the fear of annihilation in the child, although her emphasis on the destructive forces coming from *within* the child (1975: 144), as opposed to any recognition that destruction is imposed from *without*, has also significantly hindered our understanding of the abused child. Together with Freud's emphasis on Oedipal conflicts, a powerful theoretical combination was created giving credence and justification to the denial of the realities of child abuse. Shengold suggests that

> The clinical writings of some Kleinian theorists, for example, give the impression that the child's actual experiences hardly matter. There ought not to be disagreement about the question of pathogenicity of experiences as against fantasies; the crucial clinical problem is: how do experiences of overstimulation and deprivation influence the motivating fantasies of an individual.
>
> (Shengold 1979: 532)

He continues to describe how trauma creates splitting in the child:

> I am not describing schizophrenia (although in psychotic children a more destructive fragmentation of the mind can also occur in response to trauma), but the establishment of isolated divisions of the mind that provides the mechanism for a pattern in which contradictory images of the self and of the parents are never permitted to coalesce. This compartmentalized 'vertical splitting' transcends diagnostic categories.
>
> (p. 532)

Fairbairn, who worked with children who had been victims of sexual assault in the Second World War, also developed a detailed psychoanalytic model of dissociation with multiple personality as a significant feature. He argued that Freud's division into id, ego, and super-ego was only one possibility among others for a structure of the mind, and suggested that 'multiple personality is ultimately a product of the same processes of differentiation which lead to the isolation of the ego, the id and the super-ego' (Fairbairn 1952: 159). Lasky (1978) argued that multiple personality arises from developmental difficulties whereby the person can only internalize part-objects. As a result the inner world is chaotic and the person only has access to primitive defence mechanisms such as splitting, merging and projection. Multiple personality has also been considered as a variant of borderline personality (Buck 1983; Clarey *et al.* 1984), and a type of transitional object (Marmer 1980). Others have proffered other explanations from other perspectives, for example sociological role theory (Taylor and Martin 1944) and family systems theory (Beal 1978). Mitchell (1984) adopts a more political line, arguing that through multiple personality women are communicating 'simultaneous acceptance and refusal of the organization of sexuality under patriarchal capitalism' (p. 289). It can be seen that opinion is diverse, and as Brenner (1994: 83) notes in his study of recorded cases of multiple personality in one hospital:

> This condition seems to generate more controversy, confusion, and schisms in the staff than any other disorder. Reminiscent of what occurs with other primitive characters, this split is unique because the credibility of the patient and subsequently the diagnosis are often the issue . . . The dramatic quality of 'switching' to other personalities, and the obvious secondary gain of disowning one's behavior, especially when criminal charges are involved add to the controversy.

Brenner redefines dissociation as a defensive altered state, due to autohypnosis, which augments repression or splitting. This can lead to a variety of symptoms relating to alertness, awareness, memory and identity. Ellenberger (1970) examines the different ways multiple personality has been described throughout its history and identifies the following categories and description: simultaneous multiple personalities; successive multiple personalities; mutually cognizant of each other; mutually amnesic; one-way amnesic and personality clusters.

What is clear is that although multiple personality and dissociative conditions are nowadays a contentious issue, they are not new but have been the subject of serious and divided debate for a century. In more recent years this debate, particularly in the United States, has become more vocal, widespread and vitriolic, with polarized positions being adopted. As I shall show later in this chapter, this is in large part because the controversy surrounding 'false' memory has overlapped and mingled with questions relating to multiple personality. In particular, books by Putman (1989) and Ross (1989) were very significant in exploring and understanding the development of multiple personality in the context of a response to severe childhood abuse. In this country Mollon (1996) – who writes in this book – made a major contribution to the field, exploring multiple personality from a psychoanalytic perspective and from the base of having worked with patients with multiple personality.

At the same time other writers and practitioners were speaking in opposition. Essentially, these writers (Aldridge-Morris 1989 in Britain; Hacking 1995 and Spanos 1996 in the United States) argue from an iatrogenic viewpoint. That is, they argue that multiple personalities are created by therapists who actively make suggestions and who may introduce reading material to further support their diagnosis, in combination with a client who is suggestible and compliant. The patient is essentially understood as accommodating to a very particular and strongly held view of their therapist; that is, the emergence of different personalities is an iatrogenic artefact. This stance assumes a very persuasively convincing and somewhat aggressive style on the part of the therapist, who embarks on the work with a clear idea of what is wrong. The collusion of the therapist and the client encourages the false creation of personalities and this is further reinforced by media attention. This argument links the fact that personalities tend to appear in therapy, when they may not have obviously appeared before, directly owing to the persuasiveness of the therapist and the therapeutic situation. This view of the therapist as a determined detective is expressed strongly by Ofshe and Watters, who also see the therapist as actively digging for memories: 'Whether the therapist first hunts for later personalities or for repressed memories seems to vary from therapist to therapist' (Ofshe and Watters 1995: 205). They continue with this theme:

> The process of indoctrinating the client into the MPD belief system shifts into high gear after the first personality 'appears' and after the diagnosis is accepted by the client. In their descriptions of how they

'treat' the disorder once established, therapists provide a wealth of evidence that they encourage the development of alter personalities and behavior.

(p. 217)

Their line of argument has been reinforced for them by the apparently large numbers of patients being diagnosed as having multiple personalities in the United States. They, and others who dispute the validity of multiple personality, also point to what they consider to be the misuse of both drugs and hypnosis in helping patients access other personalities.

Davies and Frawley, writing from a psychoanalytic perspective, provide a different understanding of the 'alters' presenting in therapy:

It should not be surprising, therefore, that such fundamental divisions will be most likely to manifest themselves around the re-evocation of experience specific to intense transference–countertransference emergence within an on-going analysis. That such experiences are called forth only within the treatment setting by no means implies that they are created by that setting.

(Davies and Frawley 1994: 77)

Instead of viewing the therapist as a determined detective eagerly searching for detail, memories and personalities, they explore how the therapist may be inclined to do just the opposite. They describe how the therapist can resist hearing or asking about a patient's abusive history; how even nowadays, in the light of increased knowledge, they may be inclined to interpret reality as fantasy; and how patients too can be reluctant to face the horrors that they have experienced. In this scenario collusion can work the other way, with both patient and therapist preferring to hold a more favourable view of the former's world. Davies and Frawley describe the gruelling nature of work with abuse survivors and the pain of working in this area for both the participants:

Psychological trauma, especially sexual abuse, raises anxiety and discomfort within the clinician. Like society at large, a victim's family, and, frequently enough, patients themselves, therapists do not want to know that patients sitting before them were violated sexually, often repeatedly, perhaps sadistically, maybe at very young ages. We want to recoil and close our eyes to the commonness and viciousness with which children are sexually victimized.

(p. 88)

Those who oppose the iatrogenic viewpoint tend to take this stance, emphasizing that in general therapists are not searching either for histories of abuse or for evidence of multiple personality and in fact may defend themselves against seeing and hearing awful histories of abuse.

The question of 'false memory' and the validity of memory

Nowadays memory is a central aspect of any discussion on working with abuse survivors, and with multiple personality the questions surrounding this become even more complex. As Paul Antze (1996: 7) says, 'It would be safe to say that for all multiples in therapy today, memory is a central obsession. In fact, while memory is central to anyone's life story, for multiples it is usually the subject of the story.'

The extract from Ofshe and Watters quoted previously demonstrates how the debate around multiple personality has become inextricably linked to the issues of 'false memory syndrome' and to the whole complex question of memories and their accuracy in the field of trauma. With multiple personality not only is there the question of amnesia and recovering memories but many more layers are involved. If we take the view that in multiple personality the dissociation is so great that the resulting splits take on a life of their own, forming distinct personalities within the one person, it is also apparent that these identities have memories of their own. If the splitting was an unconscious attempt to render the intolerable tolerable by diffusing the experiences through sharing them, some very terrible memories must be held, and beginning to reclaim and gather these together could be very shocking. As Ellenberger (1970, cited above) has pointed out, amnesia among the personalities can be very complex: one personality may hold memories only known to itself; another may share memories with a certain specified personality or personalities and not others; and a personality may be amnesiac in its own right. The possibilities are considerable and it is not surprising that those who work in this field can find themselves in something that feels chaotic. As it is the debate rages about whether memories can be repressed and later recovered, and whether memories can be falsely implanted. It is therefore perhaps inevitable that the stakes are raised when examining this degree of intra-psychic confusion.

There is currently a heated debate over the veracity of recovered memories of abuse, with generally a major difference of opinion displayed between practising clinicians and experimental psychologists. With some exceptions each group tends actively to challenge the views of the other. Clinicians (Harvey and Herman 1994; Olio 1994) tend to trust what they see and hear from clients, and defend themselves against charges of being suggestive, tending to believe that memories can be lost and later recovered. They dispute research findings on memory – one argument being that these findings are limited to ordinary memories and that those relating to trauma are not open to laboratory experiment. Experimental psychologists (Dawes 1994; Lindsay and Read 1994) take the opposite view, challenging what they see as anecdotal clinical material and stressing the power of suggestion in creating memories. To put it simply, each group accuses the other of bias, albeit in different forms. Others avoid this dichotomy of view, and after careful and serious analysis of both research and clinical findings conclude that both recovered memories and the implantation of memories are possible (Schooler, Bendiksen and Ambadar 1997).

I have written in more detail about this controversy elsewhere (Walker 1996) but briefly, the term 'false memory' was originally coined in the United States of America after a woman, Jennifer Freyd, recovered memories of childhood sexual abuse while in therapy. Her parents disputed the accuracy of her memories and in conjunction with Ralph Underwager started the False Memory Syndrome Foundation (FMSF). I challenge the term 'false memory syndrome' as inaccurate and misleading. It implies that memories *are* false; and the use of 'syndrome' suggests a thoroughly researched, scientifically documented and proven condition, backed by controlled clinical trials – this is certainly not so with false memory. Underwager can also be challenged for his public support of paedophilia as a responsible choice:

> Certainly it is responsible. What I have been struck by as I have come to know more about and understand people who choose paedophilia is that they let themselves be too much defined by other people . . . Paedophiles spend a lot of time and energy defending their choice. I don't think a paedophile needs to do that.
>
> (Underwager 1993: 3)

Perhaps the motives of a man who publicly makes such statements are open to serious question. The British False Memory Society was set up in 1993 by Roger Scotford, who had been accused by his two daughters of sexually abusing them in childhood. These groups are adamant that therapists plant false recollections in their clients and that the lives of innocent families are consequently ruined. As with critics of multiple personality, false memory proponents claim that therapists have their own agendas; that they are unscrupulous and persuasive and that they foster unhelpful and unnecessary over-dependence:

> Even considering the substantial influence the therapist wields, there is considerable evidence that the dependence that recovered memory patients develop on their therapist is much greater than it is in other therapy settings. Again and again in the literature, recovered memory experts recommend that patients seek, and that therapists forge, extremely close emotional ties in therapy.
>
> (Ofshe and Watters 1995: 111)

One of the difficulties in responding to a highly polarized position, such as that taken up by Ofshe and Watters, is that there is a temptation to become similarly polarized; and there is some evidence in the literature that this is indeed what occurs. My own sense is that although there may be some counsellors and therapists with their own agendas, who can be suggestive and inappropriate, this does not in the United Kingdom constitute a 'movement'. I know no one in this country who describes themselves as a recovered memory therapist although nowadays all would be familiar with this concept. For most therapists, dealing with abuse is part of their normal work load and is not something that is actively sought out. In my own experience I have come across only two unrelated incidents where in my opinion the therapist has been inappropriate and suggestive and in one – the first I describe – I suspect a clear agenda to have been in operation. This involved a 'counselling' group (although all the 'counsellors' were in fact untrained or poorly trained) attached to a small evangelical church which had to my knowledge been the subject of some concern to more mainstream churches in the locality. The 'treatment' one young woman was given – verified by several sources – was reminiscent of brainwashing. She did accuse her father of abuse, and this appeared at least partially related to her 'treatment'. She moved in with one of the families actively involved in the group and had no more contact with her family, who disputed her allegations. It is not possible to know the truth of this – perpetrators do deny abuse – but certainly this group behaved unethically and inappropriately.

In another instance I worked with a young man who had been told by a previous therapist in a very early session that all his symptoms pointed to sexual abuse by his father in his earliest years. This was clearly a gross assumption. It may or may not have been accurate, but it should not have been made. In my work with him it was clear that he had suffered very well-remembered sexual abuse by his uncle from the ages of 10 to 13. His uncle had also abused other children and this was well known within the family. However, although this client came from a chaotic, un-boundaried family, with highly volatile parents who could behave entirely unpredictably both within the family and in the wider world, it was not possible to know definitely about early abuse. There is not the space here to go into detail, but our work focused on helping him to cope with the *not* knowing; on how to lead his current life as he wished to; on how to deal with the effects of the abuse by his uncle and how to manage his family concurrently. They continued to be chaotic, unpredictable and occasionally dangerous, and he – while wishing to protect himself – wanted to find some way of maintaining some relationship with them, while coming to terms with the inherent limitations to this. In my experience, abuse survivors abused within the family are far more likely to be tussling with how the relationship with them can be salvaged rather than how to denounce them publicly. Both these examples show how practitioners can be incompetent, misguided and potentially dangerous, although in my experience such practitioners are in a minority. Of course bad practice should always be challenged and taken seriously, but it should not be used as a basis for generalizations. The example of the young man I worked with also shows how clients are not simply passive objects of therapeutic intention: in this example he chose to leave this therapist, being himself unhappy about her diagnosis.

False memory proponents dispute that trauma may cause amnesia, although in disputing this they generally stay firmly within the confines of memories of childhood sexual abuse. There is considerable work on the effects, including amnesia, of other traumatic experiences – for example in relation to victims of the holocaust (Langer 1991), other war victims (Kardiner and Spiegel 1947) and other forms of violence (Gelles and Strauss 1998). The false memory groups also emphasize that therapists involved in this work see recovering memories as an end in itself. They perceive clients as essentially gullible, persuadable, easy to convince. Again there is some truth in the latter: some abused children believe that compliance with the perpetrator has saved them from worse abuse, and therapists have to be extremely careful that this pattern is not reflected and repeated in the therapeutic process.

A premise also exists that memories are recovered in therapy, the client having been unaware of them previously. Therefore, the argument goes, there is a causal link. In January 1995 the British Psychological Society produced a report that is carefully written, steers a middle course, and avoids the emotive language often heard or read in discussions on recovered memory. It noted that most public attention is concerned with memories recovered in therapy, but in fact most clinicians working in this field are counselling survivors coming to them with memories of abuse, often verified by another person. Of those practitioners questioned 90 per cent had seen sexually abused clients in the last year; a third had seen clients who had recovered memories before therapy; and about 20 per cent had seen at least one client who had in the previous year recovered a memory of abuse. However, a third also reported clients recovering a memory of a traumatic experience other than abuse. This last statement is particularly interesting: this a highly relevant area that is often not explored sufficiently.

The British Psychological Society report concludes that most abuse survivors enter therapy with memories, and this is echoed elsewhere – for example by Christine Courtois (1997). My clinical experience also reflects this: some memories are clear while others may be hazy, and placing them accurately in terms of timing and precise detail may not be possible – as with other childhood memories that may be essentially accurate but not so in their precise detail. The main events are frequently clear and often verified by other people, particularly in the case of survivors who were taken into care as a result of the abuse, or where prosecution of the perpetrator resulted. Sometimes when memories do apparently return this is not always as clear cut as it seems. A survivor who had appeared initially to have few memories later explained to me that he had always had clear memories, as had his siblings who were also abused, but that he had told me differently until he trusted me more. Indeed, some survivors nowadays are frightened of talking about their memories at all: they fear that their therapist or others they tell will think they have invented them. When memories are recovered it would be arrogant to assume that therapy in itself and by itself is the only causal factor involved. The picture is considerably more diverse. Other factors trigger memories for survivors: life becoming more stable so what previously seemed intolerable may now be tolerated; being in a trusted relationship where support is available; the birth of a child, or a child reaching the age when the survivor was abused; and the perpetrator dying. These can all have a profound effect and clinical examples abound. An example of the latter is given by a survivor: 'I find it very difficult to talk about my father. I refuse to acknowledge him. The only positive thing I can say is that he's dead . . . I couldn't have remembered the abuse when he was alive. It only came back when he was dead' (Walker 1992: 86).

Amnesia, and the consequent potential for recovering memories, can feature in the work with abuse survivors, but has become over-emphasized by the controversy surrounding this debate. It is only one aspect of work that is many layered: it may be of central concern for some clients, less so for some, and not at all for others.

Contrary to claims by false memory groups, there is evidence to support both the loss of memories of childhood abuse and the later recovery of these. Two of the studies which demonstrate this are Herman and Schatzow (1987) and Williams (1992). In Herman and Schatzow's study memories of childhood abuse, whether recovered in therapy or prior to it, were fully corroborated in 75 per cent of cases. In Williams's study the group of women in question all had documented histories of childhood abuse but 38 per cent were amnesiac.

The distinction between ordinary memory and traumatic memory is also a significant factor. Whitfield (1995: 94) notes that there is a danger of making assumptions about the latter based on knowledge of the former:

> In their research and arguments Loftus, Holmes and others . . . appear to have tried to mix apples and oranges. They have attempted to prove the non-existence of repression by studying ordinary memory and forgetting whilst not focusing on the traumatic kind. They have then tried to inappropriately transfer their findings and conclusions that ordinary memory can be modified by various influences onto a different kind of remembering and forgetting: the traumatic.

Other clinicians emphasize other perspectives in the debate: for instance Janice Haaken, a feminist psychoanalyst, warns against understanding memory in terms that are too absolute or too concrete. She feels that there is a danger in this of a survivor seeing herself, and being seen, in too narrow a context which could demean rather than free her (Haaken 1994). A further view of memories is that they are essentially constructions, and once constructed limit further understanding of the self because the self becomes defined by the memory (Markus and Nurius 1986).

Clearly memory, and how it functions, is a crucial question that must be seriously and properly studied. It is simplistic and unhelpful to think of memory as being either like a filing cabinet from which details can be neatly extracted once the door has been unlocked, or a video-recorded diary that can be replayed. There are some key questions: *do* memories hold essential truths albeit in the context of possible inaccuracy of detail? *Is* traumatic memory essentially different from other memory? *Can* memories be planted by suggestion? And is there evidence that abuse survivors *do* forget the abuse? These questions need to be kept on the agenda for ongoing examination.

Conclusion

In respect of both multiple personality and recovered memories, and recognizing that these two have become interrelated, what is needed is an openness to complexity, an awareness that at any point in history our knowledge is incomplete, and an active acknowledgement that where abuse is concerned we have been horribly wrong many times in the past. Those who have suffered from this have been those who have already suffered at the hands of perpetrators. There is a concern nowadays that families should not be subjected to false allegations, and while that is entirely valid it is crucial that it does not overshadow the major problem of child abuse and the resulting consequences for the adult survivor.

Some clinicians and others dispute that multiplicity is one of these consequences while others understand it as a comprehensible psychological response to an incomprehensible assault on the body and on the psyche. Similar questions exist in relation to memory, and while both these discussions seem at this point in time to be less polarized, with more room for reasoned debate, in the UK than they are in the US, this may yet change. Both Jenifer Antony-Black and myself are grateful to all the authors who have contributed to this book for being willing to share their views and their understanding of multiple personality, knowing as they did that our aim was to bring together in one book divergent ideas.

References

Aldridge-Morris, R. (1989) *Multiple Personality Disorder. An Exercise in Deception.* Hove: Erlbaum.

Antze, P. (1996) Telling stories, making selves, memory and identity in multiple personality disorder, in P. Antze and M. Lambek (eds) *Tense Past. Cultural Essays in Trauma and Memory.* London: Routledge.

Beal, E. W. (1978) Use of the extended family in the treatment of multiple personality, *American Journal of Psychiatry*, 135: 539–42.

Brenner, I. (1994) The dissociative character: a reconsideration of multiple personality, *Journal of the American Psychoanalytic Association*, 42: 81–9.

Buck, O. D. (1983) Multiple personality as a borderline state, *Journal of Nervous Mental Disorders*, 171: 62–5.

Clarey, W. F., Burstin, K. J. and Carpenter, J. S. (1984) Multiple personality and borderline personality disorder, *Psychiatric Clinic of North America*, 7: 89–99.

Courtois, C. (1997) Delayed memories of child sexual abuse: critique of the controversy and clinical guidelines, in M. Conway (ed.) *Recovered Memories and False Memories.* New York: Oxford University Press.

Davies, J. and Frawley, M. (1994) *Treating the Adult Survivor of Childhood Sexual Abuse: A Psychoanalytic Perspective.* New York: Basic Books.

Dawes, R. M. (1994) *The House of Cards.* Toronto: Maxwell Macmillan.

Ellenberger, H. F. (1970) *The Discovery of the Unconscious.* New York: Basic Books.

Fairbairn, W. R. D. (1952) *An Object Relations Theory of the Personality.* New York: Basic Books.

Ferenczi, S. (1955) Confusion of tongues between adults and the child, in *Final Contributions to the Problems and Methods of Psychoanalysis.* London: Hogarth Press.

Freud, S. and Breuer, J. (1895) *Studies on Hysteria.* Reprint Harmondsworth: Penguin Freud Library, Volume 3.

Gelles, R. and Strauss, M. (1998) *Intimate Violence.* New York: Simon and Schuster.

Haaken, J. (1994) Sexual abuse, recovered memory, and therapeutic practice, *Social Text*, 40: 115–45.

Hacking, I. (1995) *Rewriting the Soul. Multiple Personality and the Sciences of Memory.* Princeton, NJ: Princeton University Press.

Harvey, M. R. and Herman, J. L. (1994) Amnesia, partial amnesia and delayed recall among adult survivors of childhood trauma, *Consciousness and Cognition*, 3: 295–306.

Herman, J. L. and Schatzow, E. (1987) Recovery and verification of memories of childhood sexual abuse, *Psychoanalytic Psychology*, 4: 1–14.

James, W. (1890) *The Principles of Psychology.* Reprint New York: Dover, 1950.

Janet, P. (1889) *L'Automatisme psychologique.* Paris: Baillière.

Kardiner, A. and Spiegel, H. (1947) *War, Stress and Neurotic Illness.* New York: Hoeber.

Klein, M. (1975) *Envy and Gratitude and Other Works: 1946–1963.* London: Hogarth Press.

Langer, L. (1991) *Holocaust Testimonies: The Ruins of Memory.* New Haven, CT: Yale University Press.

Lasky, R. (1978) The psychoanalytic treatment of a case of multiple personality, *Psychoanalytic Review*, 65: 353–80.

Lindsay, D. S. and Read, J. D. (1994) Psychotherapy and memories of childhood sexual abuse: a cognitive perspective, *Applied Cognitive Psychology*, 8: 281–338.

Markus, H. and Nurius, P. (1986) Possible selves, *American Psychologist*, 41: 954–69.

Marmer, S. S. (1980) Psychoanalysis of multiple personality, *International Journal of Psychoanalysis*, 61: 439–59.

Mitchell, J. (1984) *Women: The Longest Revolution*. New York: Pantheon.

Mollon, P. (1996) *Multiple Selves, Multiple Voices. Working With Trauma, Violation and Dissociation*. Chichester: Wiley.

Ofshe, R. and Watters, E. (1995) *Making Monsters: False Memories, Psychotherapy and Sexual Hysteria*. London: André Deutsch.

Olio, K. A. (1994) Truth in memory, *American Psychologist*, 49: 442–3.

Prince, M. (1906) *Dissociation of a Personality*. New York: Meridian, 1957.

Prince, M. (1914) *The Unconscious*. New York: Macmillan.

Prince, M. (1919) The psychogenesis of multiple personality, *Journal of Abnormal Psychology*, 14: 225–80.

Putman, F. W. (1989) *Diagnosis and Treatment of Multiple Personality Disorder*. New York: Guildford Press.

Ross, C. (1989) *Multiple Personality Disorder. Diagnosis, Clinical Features and Treatment*. New York: Wiley.

Schooler, J., Bendiksen, M. and Ambadar, Z. (1997) Taking the middle line: can we accommodate both fabricated and recovered memories of sexual abuse? in M. Conway (ed.) *Recovered Memories and False Memories*. New York: Oxford University Press.

Shengold, L. (1979) Child abuse and deprivation: soul murder, *Journal of the American Psychoanalytic Association*, 27: 533–59.

Spanos, N. P. (1996) *Multiple Identities and False Memories. A Sociocognitive Perspective*. Washington, DC: American Psychological Association.

Taylor, W. S. and Martin, M. F. (1944) Multiple personality, *Journal of Abnormal Social Psychology*, 49: 135–51.

Underwager, R. (1993) Interview: Holida Wakefield and Ralph Underwager, *Paidika, the Journal of Paedophilia*, 3: 1.

Walker, M. (1992) *Surviving Secrets: The Experience of Abuse for the Child, the Adult, and the Helper*. Buckingham: Open University Press.

Walker, M. (1996) Working with abuse survivors: the recovered memory debate, in R. Bayne, I. Horton and J. Bimrose (eds) *New Directions in Counselling*. London: Routledge.

Williams, L. (1992) Adult memories of childhood abuse: preliminary findings from a longitudinal study, *The Advisor, Journal of the American Professional Society on the Abuse of Children*, 5(3): 19–20.

Chapter 2

Liza's story

Liza is a woman aged 29. She is married and has three young children from previous relationships. She was an only child and was physically, sexually and emotionally abused by her father and by other men, both as a child and within adult relationships. Her mother knew of some of the abuse but was unable to intervene to protect her daughter. Liza remains in regular contact with her parents who live locally and this relationship remains very problematic. She had a long period of time out of work, unable to cope because of the psychological difficulties she was experiencing. However, recently she has started up her own small business. Her current marriage is a more successful relationship than those she has been in previously. Her husband is aware that Liza believes that she has many personalities, and is generally supportive to her.

For many years Liza did not identify herself as multiple personality, although as will become clear from her account she was aware of different parts of her self. For the sake of clarity it will be helpful for readers to know that Liza has always had snippets of memories about her abuse but has recently been able to begin to gather them together. At 18, with the emergence of a personality called Dudley, Liza experienced the resurfacing of further memories which then became repressed until they were retriggered by the death of her best friend ten years later. Her initial awareness that there was something called multiple personality came when she read a book on the subject. At that time she strongly resisted any possibility that this could exist or apply to her. The personalities started to emerge more clearly when she was in a group for the survivors of sexual abuse, when she started talking about the different personalities, in particular talking about Tracey and her feeling that Tracey had died because of Jason's (her best friend's) death. She then herself recognized that she had multiple personalities.

She tells her story herself. It is reproduced accurately below, using her own terminology and with very few alterations. Particular care has been taken to retain

Liza'a own use of tenses – whether past, present or future, and also to retain her own use of personal pronouns: so 'I', 'we', 'she', 'it', are included as Liza spoke them. Readers may find this confusing but it reflects Liza's experience of her many selves. It is important to note that this self-description of her and her life is a snapshot in time, based upon interviews with her at specific points in her life. It is evident to the editors that the snapshot changes as time goes on, with some personalities merging with others and some being recalled and described some times, but forgotten at others. It will be noted that Liza refers to medical reports: she recently accessed her medical notes in an attempt to piece together her own history. The italics in the script are editorial, to clarify points.

Readers might like to know that as this book has progressed, Liza has had the opportunity of reading, reflecting and commenting on the various contributions.

Childhood

It was physical abuse, sexual and emotional but physical and emotional is the one I remember most – that has stopped with me. At this point I get a block on what I'm going to say and somebody else takes over. I was raped when I was 4 and I've only recently had this memory. Being touched makes me feel vulnerable and little again. Sometimes I can't bear to feel attractive because if I like myself too much then there's something wrong with me. I can't bear eye contact and I know that's because my father always stared at me. I suppose I spent most of my childhood looking at the floor. Since the age of 10 I've always felt dirty and a need to be clean – a kind of desperate need. It's such desperation you can't express it. I was never allowed to cry as a child. I remember being left alone a lot and waking up when I was little and the house being all dark. That has always resurfaced when I'm alone. I think that's sad – I can't imagine letting my children feeling that unsafe or that desperate. Sometimes when the feelings come up now I think well I'm not little, I'm not going to be scared, I'm going to help myself, but it doesn't work yet – it's like it's happening all over again.

I often wonder how a 2-year-old baby got cystitis but that's on the doctor's notes, unless it was the stress of screaming in the garage – being locked in the garage at night. God knows what the baby has got to say. It's just beyond comprehension. What gets me so much is that apparently it was a recommendation from the doctor – if it's getting to you that much and you can't get any sleep just stick her in the garage, she won't come to any harm. I've never felt the need with my three to put them anywhere like that.

Until I left home I'd have a shower and my father would come in and touch one, or you could never have a bath without him coming in and staring. When I was younger I'd go into the living room because I'm scared and I've had a bad dream and he puts his hand up my nightie and starts rubbing my bum and I remember standing there feeling horrible and frozen and my mum would just look at me and look away, and I'd be thinking, mum, will you tell him to stop but she just turns away. Now I'm starting to find out there's more underneath those memories. Everything is just one big mess.

Having friends round – I could never have friends to stop because my dad would have done it to them – he'd make comments about their breasts and try to touch them and so I got scared and stopped them coming. You're scared to stop at home and then if people invited me to their house I got scared to go there and I didn't know why I was scared. I never liked anyone else's dad – I thought all dads were the same. It invades everything and it still does even in my own house today as an adult – my dad and my mum get away with anything in the house, they just run everything.

The more you think about it the more really shitty it was, all of it. I remember being in bed once and it was May Day and I could hear people talking in the kitchen and my father came into the bedroom and said your cousin David's died and I started crying and he said you needn't fucking start crying – I've got enough with your mother. And he was my favourite cousin – we were like brother and sister. It was the same when other people died and then you tend to think that everybody dies – whoever you like dies, and a lot of them have. And that's instilled into one of them – what's the point of getting close to anyone in case they die.

It's being so scared of one individual that even when they're not in the house you can't do things. I could hear his voice shouting even when he wasn't in the house. I never got away with things that other kids do. The emotional abuse made everything so unpredictable you never know where you stand. So you don't trust anybody; you don't know what's right and wrong. I grew up with a religious mother and I think Satan himself was father's: it was like godliness in the daytime and evil at night, and then you wonder why you're confused. So on the one hand as a child I'm being took to confession when I haven't done anything wrong, and there you've got dad doing exactly what he wants when he wants and nobody says anything, and that doesn't matter because that's dad.

I used to wet the bed until I was 14 and 15. I was late telling the time – dad used to sit me on his knee and get so angry because I didn't get it – but I couldn't understand it because I was too scared of what he was going to do if I didn't get it. It's being brought up in a different world – it's one big lie. Both parents tell different lies and you don't know where you are. You just sit there and watch the world go by and keep your gob shut. There's no point in saying anything – you grow up just trying to please all the time. Somebody in there doesn't give a shit and could say what they wanted, probably Tracey and then there's someone who is really scared, and scared they're going to end up in hospital if they say anything – dad will come round and give her a good hiding, and there's someone in there that says if you deal with it; if you break free, you're going to be alright, but they're a bit distant at the minute.

Mum tried – she ran around the country with me with my dancing but then I think if all that hadn't been going on I wouldn't have wanted to do the dancing. It was like a big game and there's a few fed up with playing, well I think they all are but some can't face dealing with it. It's all beyond reason because I – whoever I is – just doesn't understand it, how anybody could even leave a 5-year-old by themselves all night. I just don't get it and as for the rape – well, I don't understand it. And then they have the nerve to criticize the way you're living and bringing up your own children, or the way you dress. I remember once, I'm not sure who it was, but one of the personalities came home in a rage about something and she smashed the bedroom up and I remember dad sitting in the living room shouting 'she's only smashing it up because she's knobbing him. And she don't like it'. It was all those kind of comments all the time even when I was little, 12 or 13.

Maimie was sitting in the kitchen one night and he came in and tripped over her boots. Maimie made a joke out of it and then he tried to strangle her and me mother just sits there saying don't do that. I remember once my dad tried to strangle my mother and I was just screaming for her and I got told to shut up and go into the bedroom. She plays games with him now all the time and I'm bored with playing. It's not fair that you have to go all through that and then relive it later on. I could have ended up in hospital; I could have killed myself and it's still happening. I don't know how I managed to survive it really. Since the rape memory it's been like, right, either you can go with your mum and dad and side with them, or you can side with her – you can believe the rape and you've got to do something about it; you've got to stick up for her and for the others. It's a bit like they're saying you sort out your mum and dad and stop them scaring us and we'll tell you the rest. Like 'you believe us first and then we'll come up with the rest of it'. That's how it feels but it's just getting the courage up to do it.

When I was in labour with my first baby when I was 19 my dad wanted me to have an abortion and I wasn't going to. I knew who the father was, he was white and we'd split up. All the way through the pregnancy my dad was saying I bet that fucking thing's black, I'll bet you that kid comes out black. I remember in labour thinking please don't let this baby be black, he'll kill me. Yet I knew it wouldn't be – it's like not trusting yourself, it's like I was so scared of him – fear is instilled into you. When I lived at home with my father we were never ever allowed to have a fire on, no matter what the weather. But we used to have it on sometimes, and we'd know when he was coming in and we'd switch it off an hour before. But he used to catch us out he'd come home and put his hands on the fire bars to see if it had been on. If it was still warm, he'd give us a good hiding and even now I can't put the fire on in my house. Because my husband at the moment doesn't like the fire on because it makes him feel a bit wheezy but I'll sit there shivering and think I'd love to put that fire on and I can't, just something stops me doing it, like the fear is still there. Sometimes I do put it on and I have to laugh to myself but it's not very often

– if I put the fire on I think the whole world is going to fall on me or something. It's really strange.

Ongoing effects of the abuse

I have nightmares – recurring nightmares that are very real when you are having them. I have stages of that – really horrific nightmares about vomiting blood, phlegm and hair, more hair and yet more hair, out of my mouth. And I can't learn to drive. I know that I switch at the wheel, somebody must switch and I can't drive. I start to get all tingly, I start to dissociate at the wheel. I was doing quite well learning to drive but that started at about the eighth lesson. I have got a very abusive driving instructor who used to bring sex in all the time. All the time I was with him I just used to think I've got to get away from him but I never did so that happened and got me out of it.

There's lots of fears and things and you don't know where they originated. I can't go into toilets and lock it. I'm always panicking if I'm going anywhere – like have I got the right time and the right day. I have to keep backtracking to make sure I have. Also all my life I've just gone from chaos to chaos to chaos – bad relationships, bad relationships and more bad relationships. Just incapable of looking after myself and doing what I want to do, or even knowing what I want to do. Half the time I don't know. And just having no good judgements of things. Alcoholism is a definite effect – I drank from the age of about 14 right up to a year ago, to the point where I was drinking a bottle of whisky a night and I thought either you give it up or else you're going to die. That was the choice.

At the moment life is a nightmare, I've been getting all these memories coming up. I have had panic attacks – as long as I can remember I've had panic attacks to the point where I couldn't go out of the house. I've never understood why they come about or when, I could never make any connection. I used to have them in crowded places. I had three in one day and then three years ago I got put on medication. When I came of it I decided to just sit there and see what happened – I just stopped being scared – I was fed up, and I thought well I'm not going to fight it any more. Once I did that the memories came, and the nightmares and things, like that's what the panic attacks were about. My hope is that once I get the memories through that I won't have any more panic attacks. It got worse after Jason my best friend died.

Another one is feeling dirty. I'm always in the bath. It's not as bad as it used to be but it's still there, I feel dirty all the time, I don't feel clean. It's like something is going to burst out of you, it's just a horrible feeling. There's a lot of physical things that are results of the abuse. Like pains in my vagina, I sat there last night and had a feeling like I was going to wet myself, or something was going to come out – it was really scary. I'm thinking to myself, it's a memory, it's a memory but it's so real, so real. Palpitations that's another one – I've had them all my life, like my heart is going to come out of my body. Shaking is another one, I'm always shaking and trembling – it's like living on the edge all of the time and you don't why. People say do an anxiety class, do relaxation but it doesn't work, not really. You've got to know why you're like this to stop this.

Another effect is always being at the doctor's with one thing or the other, not knowing why things happen, why I have the panic attacks, why I can't eat – I have stages where I can't eat anything, the longest was ten days I've gone without eating – I just can't put the food in my mouth. So my weight is either right up or right down. I've been tested for everything that you could possibly have but nothing has ever come up.

Other things I think are a direct result of the abuse too, like picking at my skin and self-mutilation. It started when I was 13 and it's never stopped. I can sit in front of a mirror and pick and pick and pick until my face is red raw and all these spots are bleeding, and all my back I'll do and then I'll have a bath and then I'll think, 'Christ, why did you do that.' I just hate myself for doing it, it looks so horrible and it hurts. I still do that to this day – I did yesterday – to my shoulders and my back and I think stop it, but there's a real need to do it.

I remember when it started – I used to get really angry with my father – I used to hate him. It's like there is so much hate in there and I was at home and I couldn't show it. I'd do it [*hurt myself*] in the mirror and me dad would be watching me from the living room, through the crack in the door. He'd shout things like 'I know what you're doing, just pack it in' and I'd just think 'no, no, shit to you' and also it was me stopping Mands getting angry.

I'm happiest when I'm pregnant – my skin always clears up and everything. I used to think it was because I'd got something to look forward to and also I couldn't go out and do things like nightclubbing. For some reason something stops when I'm pregnant. Now it's either a different self takes over and is more in the body and that person I like, that's possibly what it is. But you can't keep on having children just to feel good for nine months. As soon as I've had the baby something else takes over and then it's like I'm happy with the baby but it's selfish, it's all mine – the baby is mine and no one else can touch it, more so than other mothers I've met. I'm over-protective and it's like I go into a different world once the baby is born – my own little world with this baby, nobody else exists. That goes on quite a while.

With my children, I'm not consistent with them. It's not knowing what is abuse and what is not; what is appropriate and what isn't. I have a hard time disciplining my children because I just see them as little and vulnerable. I used to smack quite a bit and I used to get terrible rages and scream and shout and I had to stop doing that and now I'm the complete opposite, I'm too soft and that can cause problems with your partner. I just don't want the children to feel like I used to feel – I never felt safe, I was always scared and I have a hard time knowing what's right and what's wrong for the children.

When I couldn't open the front door the other week whoosh, all the old feelings came up, the fear, and that's the little 'un because she feels trapped, but I was in the memories at that time so I couldn't really piece it together but I know that kind of feeling of being trapped, or public toilets where there's a couple of doors to go out through that's where something happens – I lose time or memory because I can go into a toilet and then not remember how to go out – say there's a cleaning door and another door there is a panic that takes over like a trapped feel.

The different selves

The littlest is about 6 months old. Then we've got a 5-year-old – I know she doesn't like the dog and gets scared on her own in the house. Three or four weeks ago I became aware of the little 'uns, but having said that all of their fears have always been there. But it's odd, lying there on the settee and watching another version of yourself going upstairs, and then you open your eyes and you're actually sitting on the settee – that was scary.

Then there's Godspell – she's 14. I've had a few more memories about her. She did a couple of musicals but she also went to a local stage school for a year or so and she was a witch in *Macbeth*. Then we've got Dudley who's 18 and gay or bisexual – attention seeker is what's been said about her. She likes to dress outlandishly; like punky; quite aggressive but she's not into punk music. She lived with a woman for a couple of years but that ended abusively. Her doctor's report is psoriosis, high temperatures, sore throat, coughs when socializing and panic attacks – she wanted to go in the army but was rejected because of this. Dudley used to suffer from nightmares and I believe that was stuff trying to resurface and it didn't get a chance. She was hit by partners in gay relationships. Dad tried to strangle her and after that she left home. She's into spiritualism. She left home and started a new life on the gay scene that lasted a few years. She liked the gay scene because she can have men on the gay scene as very good friends without any sexual involvement, she can have cuddles and stuff and there's no threat. She doesn't eat; she wants to be really thin; she doesn't like families.

Then there's Maimie – I've no idea how old she is. She was around for the first pregnancy, because she's the one who got pregnant. Maimie is bisexual and she's Jason's best friend. She drinks and drinks and drinks and doesn't know when to stop. She's a bit arrogant. But she doesn't pick her skin though. She's probably more of a clown. She was there for the first pregnancy and Joan for the next two. The first pregnancy was a bad nine months being on my own and things trying to resurface. Things went missing at times – so someone else was there, either the 5-year-old or Joan – they both hide things. Things were quite scary – when the baby was a few weeks old and needed feeding don't ask me who fed her in the night because I didn't. I've got no knowledge, no memory but someone did and wrapped it all back up. Someone else took over – I used to put it down to ghosts.

Then we have Mands – I think Mands is a boy. Mands – she surfaces, or tries to, quite a lot. She's quite destructive and angry and turns it inwards; she picks her skin, doesn't like anything, is never happy. She came into being when I was 13 and resurfaced again at 15. She makes me feel like I'll lose my husband and not to trust. Sometimes I'll want to wear nice clothes and she'll make sure I can't by picking at my skin and makes it a mess. She does have a few months off in the summer because that's when I get in the sun and then she can't do anything about it. So in summer it's different as long as I get the sunshine – I get tanned, and look better and feel better and more confident. She had girlfriends at 13. Her GP's records say – acne, hospital skin clinics – but making herself bleed is self-inflicted. Things I remember about Mands – is psychological abuse from Dad; being scared all the time, being touched in the shower and in other places in the house, him making sexual comments about me. She has the first real boyfriend and him [*boyfriend*] trying things on with her and her getting a feeling of not really being there when he's doing it. She smokes, sucks her thumb and drinks, that's when drinking and getting drunk started. I know when she's around because I hate myself. Her skin gets sore – the feelings come out in the skin; she hates religion and she has always hated her dad. A furious temper if it was let out – I don't dare to let her temper out because there's so much hate in there.

Some of the selves are aware of the others. Like Mands is aware of Tracey – I've always known I've been Mands – self-destructive but I never knew why or understood it. I've known Tracey has been there for years but it's not neat and tidy because they all resurface – I can see that Mands resurfaced throughout adulthood and Joan does and Tracey does. Tracey is 17 and she took over from Mands when I was 15 when sex became an issue; when she felt she had to start getting involved in sex. Her doctor's report says she gets stomach pain but nothing is found. It's difficult [*being clear about medical records*] because they were alongside one another so you don't know which is going to the doctor's. She was raped and hit by various relationships. She gets drunk; is promiscuous. She's a good laugh and she's feminine. Mands liked sweatshirts and jeans, Tracey is the mini skirt type and has a sarcastic sense of humour. She's changed – her dress is getting more sophisticated. We can't work out how she has fun any more because she used to drink and go clubbing and we don't do that any more. It's like if you can't deal with something she pops up and she'll turn it into humour – we'll have a laugh about it, but she can also be like 'I'm not taking this, shove off' – quite strong like that. So with her, since I was 15 I've been aware there's someone else.

Tracey seems to resurface any time there is a new relationship. She pops up – Tracey's taste in men is a bit sad really – her first husband was really the twin of her father. I don't know whether someone else chooses the husband and then Tracey takes over for a bit. I quite like Tracey. She's quite good at getting men and having fun, but then it starts getting a bit too much because there are children and you can't always be out clubbing and she starts to die off a bit. She needs entertaining all the time; needs thrills. Tracey drinks as well. She's not too hot on being a mother either – she'd rather be out than being at home.

So there's a few arguments that come out of that. Especially when Tracey has a bloke and then there's a switch and someone else comes in who says 'who's this? Oh oh, get rid of him – we don't need this.' Then there's another one but I don't know about her – she's 29; she could possibly be the counsellor or the detective. She's the one who went to college and did all these psychology courses, so she was possibly the one who was delving in to find out what was going on. She's the one that married. Like a test really – you're supposed to be with a nice man and not be hit, so why can't you do it, so we'll marry one and see what happens. She was the one who wanted to find out why she couldn't handle love or affection, and why she had all of us.

College had to be stopped – I couldn't handle that any more because I didn't know what was happening, all I knew was that they used to switch in the class when difficult subject matter came up. The one that went knew a lot but the others didn't like it. There was a lot of switching going on and you could feel it in the class – you could feel it brewing within you, and a need to run out – it was absolutely terrible, feeling alienated. She was getting good grades. She's not very happy at the moment because she wants to do college work. Perhaps in the future she'll do something.

Mrs B is 23 and on the doctor's report she suffers constipation, tonsillitis, which is constant, and stomach pains. She was rushed into hospital and in the end they decided it was stubborn bowel. She gets a lot of headaches. She spent five years being a battered wife, loads of things happened to Mrs B. She got locked up in the house. Her husband nailed the windows down and put deadlocks on all the doors so she couldn't go out. He used to keep her awake at night and pull her hair out if she refused sex. One night he took the fuses out so all the house was in darkness and chased her round the house all night trying to scare her. He got a knife to her throat once as well. The list is endless – he tried to set fire to her. He threw a fryer full of hot fat at her – she had to put up with so much. She's a clean-aholic; has to bleach the whole house through and would get up at three in the morning to clean the cupboards out or hoover. Everyone thinks they are a perfect couple – no one knows what goes on inside the house.

She spends five years like that and then one day there's an argument with her husband; he threatens to throw her out the window; at some point someone pops up and smacks him round the face and I think that was Sparkie. They'd had enough. It was a mistake; he beat her worse and she called the police. They weren't willing to help unless she got a court injunction but she had to stop in the house with him until it arrived so that wasn't an option. They didn't even tell her there was such a thing as a women's refuge, so she didn't know there was anywhere else to go.

Sparkie is 27: she starts getting palpitations; loses weight. The doctor told her she was depressed. She was put on anti-depressants and does psychotherapy and that's when things start to change. She realizes that her husband doesn't have to have that kind of control so she leaves. She goes to college; makes some friends, and her tutor once said she was social networking – that she was getting the foundations ready to leave him. She wasn't really conscious that she was doing it. Sparkie is the counsellor type person; intellectual; political. Her husband stopped hitting her for three months but she knew it was coming and that when it came it would be bad, so she took the kids and went into a refuge.

Sparkie had panic attacks – she was the one who had a mental background and she was classed as agoraphobic. Then this new self came in when the panic attacks stopped. She's the one who goes to the sexual abuse project [*where she attended a group*]. She's only been here about a year, or perhaps two years ago because she's the one who knows there's something wrong inside. She could be about 28. She had a mental breakdown when Jason died. It felt then like the stuff that Dudley tried to resurface at 18 came up – it didn't get a chance then but it did with the new self. She went through a phase of doing meditation; stopped drinking and she becomes aware of the dreams and that they mean something, and that's when she becomes aware of the other personalities. She's only had three good months since she became created when she's felt relaxed and not scared. When she first started doing meditation she used to see things but realized it was Nadia doing her dancing. It's like I had a few nice things in my head before the bad things started to come up.

Then there's Billie – I don't know much about her but she doesn't like holidays. She did the first day at school and holidays: until about 16 she always went on holiday. Now she tries to stop the holidays and last time she didn't go. I think she gets quite jealous. I didn't know anything about her until recently. She's always been in there but I don't know what she does apart from getting scared and feeling trapped. Billie is 4 and was raped in bed from behind and I've had that memory. The doctor's report for Billie was coughs and colds. Billie has always been about though I didn't know who it was – and with her I get feelings: certain fabrics on my skin remind me of the nightie I had on the night of the rape and trigger feelings. I get a terrible smell with those memories, and she resurfaces later and re-enacts what I believe is all the abuse on other children – she acts out sex on the teddy bear and is left feeling guilty like when she was raped – it's horrible.

After Billie remembered being raped at 4 and being alone in the house and in the garage I'd got so much going on in my brain with the older ones – they were all saying different things and that's when the writing started [*all the personalities keep their own journals*]. As soon as I've written everything down that they wanted to write it all started to become clearer. I started to piece them together in terms of their history and so on. Making models of the different selves has been helpful – I knew which they were and I knew there was a gap. [*Liza has created models of the different personalities.*] It helps when it all gets too bad and I can look at them and think that's me, I was once like that, I was a baby, I was little – it's a way of trying to look at yourself again. It's like they come out of my head and are there in front of me. I'm not sure who makes them. But it's quite scary as well. You've got to learn to listen to them all and you don't know what they're going to tell you.

There is a baby who is 6 months old. The baby won't stop crying so is put on sleeping medication and this is repeated at 12 months. The baby was locked in the garage at nights because it cried so much. I've had what I believe is a memory of being in the garage and I have that memory at the same time as I have Billie's memories. I get the bad smell with that and the terror. Nadia is 7. She was treated for epilepsy twice. She complains of dizziness, she gets stomach ache and diarrhoea and is allergic to strawberries. Her memory is being left alone in the house and abused by two men outside the family. She was taken by two African men up the town. That's something I've always remembered but I didn't know who it was. She's scared of, and hates being on her own at night. She is scared of the dark. She hides things, particularly in the past. She sleepwalks and goes for windows so if I'm staying in a strange place I wake up in the night trying to get out of the window and I think that belongs to her. As a child she had accidents a lot. She does dancing; is religious and basically has the childhood. I know she had mumps but I haven't got a lot about her. She likes dogs – she's the one who has a dog. Nadia on her first communion day went to the church and set fire to her veil in front of everybody, I don't think on purpose but she was next to the candles – but they're the only memories I've got. I don't think she got into trouble for burning the veil but it was always something that was always brought up – a bit silly, a bit dopey, clumsy that type of thing. I think at the moment she is the one who suffers with all of the nose bleeds but I'm not sure.

Joan, she's 10 – she's the one that sits with my son and sucks thumbs together and cuddles noses and things like that – she's silent but creative and she's surfaced at various times in my life. She likes flannelette things and I believe resurfaces now to have babies and deals with pregnancy and leaves someone else to get on with it immediately afterwards – that's why it changes the day afterwards [*after having the baby*]. The memories are of Joan and Nadia running alongside each other and Joan takes the abuse and Nadia does day time [*is there during the day*]. Joan looks after the other ones and keeps them quiet. She was molested by somebody at her mother's work. I've got a couple of memories of it happening but I was at the workplace for seven years so I don't know how often it happened. Joan gets earache and becomes very quiet. She resurfaced when Jason died – she deals with death and trauma. I think she dealt when my grandma died. I remember coming home in the car and seeing Joan ahead in the car. I think she writes the poetry.

Joan told what was happening: she was the one that went to the doctor's. She was at the doctor's on average once every three weeks for a year with one thing and another and reading the doctor's report it was dead obvious to anyone that something was wrong. On her medical notes it says faint feelings, feeling as if she is going to fall, unusually quiet, off food and palpitations. She was given glucose tablets and anti-depressants. I've always had the memory of going to the doctor's for that. I remember those feelings. I've read them and my own doctor said he doesn't know how they missed it. He said your mum must have wanted help from keeping bringing you – she wanted someone else to deal with it. And he says that someone must have been aware of something.

Joan wrote the 'Mushroom Land', the story of a child being beaten with a leather belt and beasts coming into the bedroom at night and being locked away. She went to live in mushroom land. It's full of abuse in children's language. My mum actually typed that up for me so I find it difficult to believe that no one actually saw anything. So if she was doing that in a story at home what was she writing at school when you write about your life at home.

Joan was taken to the doctor's about every three weeks for a year then there's a three month gap in the doctor's report when I improved dramatically. That's when my father left to live with another woman and I've always remembered that. He came back in November and that's when I'm back at the doctor's again – sore throats, feeling sick, bronchitis and high temperatures. I think she's a controller and kept the little 'uns quiet and it's a bit like Armada and Mands argue over who's going to deal with things – I'm not sure but it's like Armada's the key. She controls what is being said – things like 'let's not upset anyone, let's be polite'. Armada resurfaces in later life to be happy, have good times, she sings in the school choir. She's been around but I've only just acknowledged her and the only sorts of feelings I can put with her is the feeling sick and choking feelings I get – I think they're hers. She was created to take over from Joan and do acting and singing. She wears dresses and was feminine like a little girl.

This one is when I start picking my skin – she hasn't got a name. She had a nickname of 'Spot' at school – that's what other children called her. She doesn't like herself. She draws and she might be 4 because it was at that age I started drawing. It tended to be skeletons and horrible things. When I was little I had a free expression board in my bedroom and that had vampires and devils and things. So I'm not sure if that's somebody else or not, I don't know. I will find out eventually.

Over a year ago I was sitting at the dining room table and I saw a little version of me sitting at the table and I was writing to her and I could see her sitting at the table plain as day but I thought that was dead sweet, that didn't scare me. I just thought that's me when I was little. The recent memory, when I heard footsteps coming round the bed that's something I'll never forget and that made me more aware of the little 'uns. I suppose as well I'm aware that I can do some things some time and not others. I used to be able to play the piano and read music and I can't – Joan does that – and I can't. It's like singing – I can't sing to save my life but somebody could because we had someone in a choir for two years doing it. She hasn't got a name but I should say she's 14. It's like there's one that tells me to keep quiet – some of them I know their names, I don't know others – but I know there's times when I wasn't to say something and one has shut me up. There is definitely someone in there who shuts people up. There's someone in there who wants her own way when she wants and will throw a wobbly and starts crying and has a mard. I've been trying to work on her the last couple of years – I try and tell her she's going to have to wait; like she can't have everything today.

There's one that's really sexy and seductive though she's not around any more – she got my husband hooked, it is like it was someone different did that because I can't do it. Even he's asked for that one to come back. There's somebody who gets very irritated when someone else tries to take over and that's quite a problem because like you can be needing help thinking 'I can't do this on my own', and someone comes along to help and someone else gets irritated because they're helping. One's got to do everything on her own.

They've all got their own friends and if one of them arranges to have a friend around and then isn't around when the friend shows up it's quite awkward. Trying to talk to someone when you're thinking 'who invited you because it wasn't me'. But the last few months they're isolating themselves so there isn't a problem. It feels safer because someone in there has got a very bad choice of friends and I've got to sort that one out. They've all got their own choice of dress and the things they like; their own drinks they like. One of them drinks hot milk – I think that's Joan.

I buy the older ones things – clothes and underwear and things but recently I've bought the little 'un things: the 5-year-old's got a doll's house, and the 4-year-old's got a rag doll, Nadia's got the dog – the holiday girl hasn't got anything. Joan has got three cats – she's spoilt, possibly to keep the others quiet because she looks after the younger ones. When the younger ones pop up I get her something to make it better.

I have some memories connected to a baby but I don't understand them. I don't know when the baby's about – I haven't worked that one out yet. Someone in there makes things and I assume that's Joan. I think if anyone wanted to deal with their father it would be Mands. Somewhere in there somebody gets very angry and then just starts to cry. When I let them get angry they just start sobbing and it kind of cancels the fact that you're angry – to sit there sobbing in front of the person you're angry with. They're not a bad bunch really. There's 12 altogether.

Memories and returning memories

When I was about 10 or 11 I was put on anti-depressants, quite a high dose. At a later stage about 16, I was put on valium. Last year I was put on anti-depressants; heavy tranquillizers and sleeping tablets. The last time I was put on these three drugs a few days into them I woke up in a memory and I thought that's what it's all about, it's about the abuse by this man outside of the family. Once I'd been put on the drugs I was too scared to come off them. I kept being told I had to give them time to work but I think they made things worse because the panic was there 24 hours a day. I used to watch the clock and think get through the next five minutes and you'll be alright and that's how I lived for about six months.

Before I was on the tablets it was bad but I'd get a couple of hours off – it wasn't so intense. As soon as I came off them I started to get the buzzing and the dissociation. I just decided to stick with it. First time round when I was put on all the tablets I had real bad visual stuff – I could see things in the house. Once when I had dried flowers in the house and I hadn't eaten for ten days – I was a real mess – I could see bits of what were dried flowers on the carpet and I was convinced they were ants. I could see them moving and that was scary. I didn't dare get up. I think that was the result of the medication. Everything escalated – very bad visual stuff – everything was moving in the street and I couldn't go outside.

When the memories started coming this time a few months ago it wasn't so bad as that – I didn't get the visual stuff as bad. I was a lot more aware this time and the feelings started coming. I've always had snippets of memory, memories that have always been there, but this time I started to place them together and it's really terrifying but there is such a need to know. It's like you've got a detective inside you who wants to piece it all together. And then you've got somebody there who really doesn't want to go through this – like it's saying 'I can't take any more'. And a little 'un saying 'come on and listen to me' and it is scary, and I'd have done anything to have got out of going through it. It is scary. If I hadn't some awareness of what was going on I'd have ended up being locked up because it was suggested before that I should go on a psychiatric unit. That would have made it a hundred times worse – I'm scared enough without being put in a situation where you're going to be even more scared.

In the last couple of years I have lost time, but I don't really know before then. I can't tell. But there is a bit of an argument going on about that one. Some things I do remember but I don't know why they've happened. I can get very defensive if anyone questions if I remember things or not. I don't have many memories for some of them, just holidays and things. Sometimes I get a memory and then I can get a photo and put a memory to it. Some photos I've got no memories of but I thought everyone was like that and people didn't remember things.

I can go in a shop and be all carefree and happy and think I'm all on me own and enjoying myself, buy something, come out of the shop and I've got no memory of where the bus stop is or how to get to it and that will start a panic attack. But I usually get myself out of it – somehow or another I get home. Sometimes it's about one wanting something and another saying no. I do have a terrible problem with having clothes, so someone got the arse and came out of the shop but that one didn't know where we were. I used to be able to cope with it, you don't know what it is and you just cope with it, it's normal to you. There is one space in later life that is bothering me, still bothers me now because I didn't know anything about it till me friend Jason told me about it a few years after. One night we went to a night club. I remember getting in the car to go there but I have no memories of the next couple of days. He said I picked up a bloke and brought him back, slept with him and Jason took him back to the railway station the next morning and I've got no knowledge of this whatsoever. Things like that bother me because I wonder if there is any more incidents like that. There's probably hundreds of them. I'm not sure if it's one who likes attention – you know that type – who picks blokes up and goes back with them.

The impact of living with different selves

Yesterday [*when self-harming*] I thought, go downstairs, try and find something else. I tried to draw, I tried to switch it off. I said to her; 'come on, let's see if you can draw' and she drew a fairy, she did a big fairy and I thought 'there you are you can draw a fairy, you can do that'. I did feel better after that because I found her something else to do. That's the first time I've done that. It's so difficult when you're saying to her 'let's find you something else to do'. I sat there thinking, is this going to work. Sometimes I find it more confusing because I'm having conversations with my selves, I think I've not recognized before that I'm having them, having conversations with them.

It's hard work with one voice saying this and another that and them changing behaviour and everything. I thought giving up drinking would be the worst thing but that was quite easy really – I didn't drink for about six months at all and then somebody wanted a drink so we did reach a compromise.

Decision making, that's a direct result of the abuse because it's like the different selves all want different things but I didn't realize that until recently. Even wanting a pet in the house caused such a dilemma. I wanted a cat. I wanted one when I was little, and I was never allowed to have one and it took me such a long time to get the courage up just to have a cat. Somebody wanted the cat, others didn't because it was too much responsibility, and then we had the thing that my parents wouldn't let me have an animal – that was instilled into me.

So I ended up with three cats because I wanted a Persian, someone else wanted a tabby and someone else wanted another one, and then someone wanted a dog so we had a dog. I didn't want a dog but it kept going on and going on so I got a dog. That caused trouble because in the dog sanctuary I sat crying and crying because there wasn't the dog I wanted – I felt like I'd regressed to 6. I think it was Nadia that took over because Nadia used to like dogs. She wanted to have a puppy and I wasn't going to have a puppy because they're too much trouble. So she threw a tantrum in the middle of the dog sanctuary. It lasted a couple of days and then I thought 'well you've got a dog so you've got to be happy'.

It's like inner arguments with different selves. My husband sees them all as children and at the minute that's how I see them. They are all me – they're different parts of me. I do see Tracey as separate; the others I'm not sure about. Perhaps the fear is there is going to be someone in there I don't yet know about and they're going to pop up and do something. If I know about them it's OK. Sometimes they are separate and sometimes they are not, but I'm scared of the separateness in case I go off and commit suicide or something; that I might lose control. Another part of me says there isn't someone that destructive or they'd have shown themselves by now but I don't know. When I was on medication before I wanted to go out and just kill myself, but I couldn't but somebody up there said 'why don't you just kill yourself and get done with it.' So I suppose there is someone in there like that but so far the others have taken over to make sure it doesn't happen. Once when I was younger I overdosed but not enough to do any real damage. But I never told anyone. But I don't suppose anyone would have taken any notice because I'd been telling them things all my life.

I never used to understand that I can have a wardrobe full of clothes, wake up one morning, put them all in black bags, and tip them. Then come back later with new clothes – from second hand shops and things – put them in, wake up two months later and do it all again. Like two months ago I bought this very feminine dress, brought it home, never wore it and threw it away. That's something now I wish I hadn't done. I think they've all got different tastes in clothing. I went through quite a while with one where everything was predominantly black. I think that was Tracey – she's all black with boots and things. Coats – they've all got their own coat. That's something my husband finds very irritating. If you put the wrong coat on you don't half know about it all day. I used to say at one stage if I put a bra and a dress on that I used to feel like a man in drag, that's how it felt. It's ever such a strange feeling. I think there is one male personality but I'm not sure, he hasn't made himself known but I feel it sometimes. I went through a stage where I wore boxer shorts.

I went out with a man for a year and literally you can wake up one morning and there will be somebody about saying 'I don't know what you're doing with him but we're going to get rid' and it's like there's one who's desperate to hold onto him, or a few or whatever, and an argument goes on between them.

And changing things around in the house – like you can decorate and then you have to redecorate very shortly afterwards, because it was all right for one but the one who is there now doesn't like it. And moving the living room around, constantly. Different selves haven't learnt to live in the same space yet. I've got better, they're getting on better, because now I'm more or less happy in the house, although in the last year I have redecorated the house twice right the way through. But I think it's going to stop like that.

All my life I've never bothered with bedrooms, bedrooms never had to be decorated, didn't have anything nice in them, It was just horrible, a horrible room, but that changed about a year ago and it's now one of the best rooms in the house. The living room was the one nice room in the house and somebody pointed it out and said you don't spread this niceness around the house. Someone said there aren't bits of you in every room, and I thought about it and thought the living room is the focal point. I realized you only feel good in the living room, you don't feel good in any other room and that's when I spread it out around the house. The more I think about it the more I think they all had their own hand in each room in the house, because each room has a definite characteristic. The hall way – it's foresty, so whoever likes goblins and gooks that's theirs. And the kitchen is more the feminine place – quite pretty.

There are lots of effects – it's back to consistency. Whatever you take up and do, like going to college, it's keeping the one who wants to go to college there. The others have worked. I've got one who's a nursing sort of person, she's the one that does care assistant work. Another one works in a factory. But no one works at the moment although recently there was one. I got a job but because of what was happening and the memories, I lost the job. But at that point someone wanted to go out to work. There was a definite battle going on there. Sometimes you don't feel you've slept for months, because sometimes when you do sleep you're getting bits and bobs of memory coming up all the time. I don't know whether I'll ever be able to hold down a job but I did before the memories started resurfacing.

When the new husband came along he's definitely a different man to the type I've had before, and there was a definite argument that went on for quite some time. It's still going on, as to whether to keep or get rid. It's like somebody else chose this man. Somebody usually chooses the men but this time someone else had a choice. Sometimes I look at him and it's as if I'm looking at him through somebody else's eyes. It's like when he's being all loving and nice and suddenly I'll say 'oh, just get lost'. But then there's someone in there that wants it, and it's like there is a continual argument.

Even little things like eating – there's one in there that would be a vegetarian, and then we get bored with that so we eat other things. In cups of tea someone likes sugar and someone doesn't. So I go through times of having no sugar and then it suddenly doesn't taste right.

There's a lot of pain and hurt when I see other people's parents with their grandkids – like my husband's parents; they're not ideal and a bit lacking in emotion but they'd do anything for you; they'll always help you out and you can talk to them. They don't understand but they do believe. Being believed makes all the difference. I just think this is normal. Before I realized it had a name it was just how it was, it was just how I lived. Somebody inside me went and got a book on it and brought it back. One of me didn't want to read it, one did, and that argument goes on, and that triggered the fear, because I don't experience it like it was in the book – I don't wander off for a couple of years and don't know what I'm doing. Finding out it has got a name, there's a lot of fear in that.

It is helpful too [*having many selves*] because if one can't do anything another one can do it. Before the memories started coming back they just used to get on with it on their own. One would crop up and would say, 'well you can sod off', and another one would come in. It was finding out there was something called multiple personality and the memories coming back that was frightening. I've only told a few people what I'm going through and they think it's rubbish and that puts you down. I don't know them all yet – who there is and how many there are. My husband doesn't really believe me – he believes the abuse happened but he doesn't believe there's all these different people and yet he's aware of some of them, he has seen them. I think people would just like to shove me off somewhere and give me a load of tablets. Enough people have tried including my mum.

I don't understand about integration. I don't get it, nothing goes in on that one – perhaps because they don't want it. I don't see how you get all these people to do the same and think the same. I don't understand that. It could be boring couldn't it just being able to say I think that or I do that, and that's it.

Experience of helping professions

I've only recently become aware of what the little 'uns went through but 6 weeks old you could say it started with being given something quite strong to make me sleep. I checked my medical records recently so I know that. I cried all the time and at 12 weeks old I was still being given it. I couldn't believe it when I saw I was treated for epilepsy – that was alarming. I can remember being given anti-depressants when I was 10 or 11. I remember going to the doctor's that day – I was absolutely terrified and I couldn't speak and I just had this medicine given me.

It just went on I was sent to skin clinics – it wasn't acne, I was doing it to myself and all they said at the skin clinic was just stop doing it and it won't be like that. Well if it was that easy I'd have just done it wouldn't I? I didn't know why I did it, I just had to. Later on I was put on valium – I can't remember much then but I was drinking a lot and I was put on Mogadon. I was in a right mess. Later I was sent to a psychiatrist and that experience was beyond words. I gave him a 30-minute account of my life as I knew it and I told him I was in counselling for incest and abuse and he was sitting there and doodling and not saying much. I thought how much more can I give you without you helping me. He prescribed anti-depressants and assertiveness classes. I don't think I've got a problem with assertiveness as such it's more a question of why do I get in such panics? Why was my vision blurred? Why was everything distorted – why were voices distorted?

He was absolutely useless – I just couldn't believe it. I went to see him again. He just wasn't interested – they just shove tablets down your throat. There's no point going really. There was another time when I was having blackouts and palpitations and I was sent to psychotherapy. I did six months of that and that did help. It brought out someone in me who was willing to get out and leave the husband and leave the abusive situation and she came up and I took off. I used to talk about the fears and how my husband intimidated me and somehow it clicked that I didn't have to be scared any more so I left so that was helpful.

Doctors and psychiatrists have never been any good and there's never been any recognition of multiple personality although the psychotherapist did give me a book on sub personalities. I don't know if they're the same – I don't feel they are although in some ways I identified with that. Psychiatry is right at the bottom in terms of what was helpful, although I did only have experience of the one psychiatrist and I've heard of others that are better. Some doctors are bad but my young GP at the moment is very good and he's quite aware. Counselling and psychotherapy are top of the list. I've been in a group and that helps: you hear others and it makes you realize what you've got to do, like learn to listen. And people will remind you, say, of your mum and you have to sit there and say it's not your mum and not everyone is the same. They're not all going to abuse you. Learning to listen in groups has helped me listen to the different selves in me. I'm learning to let them out because at first you think the world will fall in if you let them out, especially if one is angry.

Chapter 3

Multiple Personality Disorder: a sceptical perspective

Peter Dale

Introduction

A range of professional influences are brought to bear in writing this chapter, including nearly 25 years' experience in a variety of settings working with people with mental health problems. My original professional training was in psychiatric social work, followed by a post-graduate diploma in counselling. Following positions in child and family psychiatric departments, since 1980 I have worked for the NSPCC: first as a practitioner at the Rochdale Child Protection Team (1980–86); and latterly as the manager of NSPCC East Sussex based in Hastings. I also maintain a small private counselling and supervisory practice. My major research interests involve perceptions of helpful and unhelpful factors in the therapeutic process of adults who were abused as children (Dale 1998); and exploration of outcomes of independent assessments following serious child abuse (Dale and Fellows 1999).

NSPCC East Sussex provides an integrated range of independent assessment and therapeutic services following all forms of child abuse, including a specific counselling service for adults who were abused as children. In 11 years the NSPCC East Sussex Counselling Centre has seen over 300 adults who were abused as children. Although many have severe abuse backgrounds, none of these clients, to our knowledge, have experienced dissociative phenomena severe or chronic enough to constitute Multiple Personality Disorder (MPD).

This is not what would be expected on the basis of much of the North American literature on MPD. In view of this discrepancy, and alerted from my own research to the sorts of therapy which clients experience in negative ways (Dale *et al.* 1998), I became concerned that the field of MPD contains beliefs and practices which potentially could cause harm to adults who were abused as children. On this basis, my argument in this chapter is that controversial MPD models prevalent in North America should not be imported wholesale, without critical scrutiny, into the UK therapeutic community.

Conceptual history of MPD

Multiple Personality Disorder is a puzzling condition. Mental health professionals disagree profoundly as to its genuine nature and the extent to which it is accurately diagnosed or misdiagnosed. In this chapter I will draw attention to some of the controversial issues relating to the phenomenon, diagnosis, incidence and treatment of MPD. Readers will quickly detect my caution about considering MPD to be a naturally occurring phenomenon on a wide scale. I also question whether some of the typical treatment approaches described in the MPD field are an appropriate way of responding to typical presenting symptoms and problems.

One of the major criticisms of the idea that MPD is a widespread naturally occurring psychological disorder (invariably related to repressed memories of severe child abuse) is that the role of cultural influence is insufficiently taken into account as an explanatory factor for the ways in which the distress of particularly suggestible individuals is manifested. To understand the significance of this, it is important to consider how the current concept of MPD (individuals who believe that they have scores – or hundreds – of autonomous 'alter' personalities) has developed over time.

While the phenomenon of dual consciousness and demonic possession has been reported in religious contexts over many centuries (Rowan 1990; Mulhern 1994); secular and psychological interest is commonly dated back to the late nineteenth century and to the practice and beliefs of Charcot, Janet and Freud. This was a very important era in psychological history, and there is much that we should continue to learn from it. The pressing concern of that time was 'hysteria' – a condition predominantly affecting young women which included a wide range of vivid physical/emotional symptoms and personality problems (Piper 1996).

The eminent neurologist Jean-Martin Charcot worked at the Salpêtrière asylum for women in Paris in the late nineteenth century. There were two main groups of patients: those who suffered from forms of epilepsy, and those afflicted by 'hysteria'. At the Salpêtrière, hysteric patients were accommodated alongside those suffering from epilepsy; and the former invariably came to imitate the behaviour of the latter. In what became known as 'Charcot's circus', patients were put on public display with Charcot demonstrating how he could induce stereotypal sequences of bizarre behaviour by pressing on their ovaries (Webster 1995). Charcot's approach eventually fell into disrepute and the regime in the Salpêtrière changed. Epileptic and hysteric patients were no longer mixed together, and staff were instructed to ignore the dramatic behaviour of the hysterics. Without reinforcement, this behaviour rapidly declined, clarifying the significant contributory element of suggestibility (Shorter 1997).

Freud (who had trained under Charcot) also utilized authority and specific pressure with suggestible patients, generating the accounts of 'repressed' memories of childhood sexual abuse which his theory at that time demanded (Webster 1995). In 1886, a crucial year in psychotherapy history, Freud consequently proclaimed that repressed memories of childhood sexual abuse were the cause of hysteria and neurotic symptoms. This notion remains a matter of significant controversy over a century later. The way in which Freud developed (and rapidly abandoned) this theory is less common knowledge. In the face of recent meticulous scholarly examination of original documents (particularly private correspondence) it is difficult to avoid concluding that Freud did not develop his theories in accordance with contemporary scientific protocols. Instead, Freud developed an *a priori* intuitive theoretical notion of repressed sexual abuse, and set out to confirm this via his own 18 patients who were induced into complying with his expectations that they produce abuse-related material. Freud then prematurely proclaimed his 'discovery' to the world (Thornton 1984; Hacking 1995; Webster 1995; Crews 1998).

This is a very different picture from that previously presented by Masson (1984). Masson's influential but misleading account claimed that Freud's patients spontaneously disclosed to him memories of previously repressed abuse (the 'Seduction' theory), and that Freud (correctly) believed these accounts for a time before (erroneously) coming to see them as fantasies in accordance with his newly formulated 'Oedipal' theory. Webster (1995) comprehensively demonstrates that both the seduction and Oedipal theories represented Freud's theoretically driven speculation, rather than being reflections of actual experiences reported by his highly suggestible patients.

Another important lesson from the era of psychological responses to hysteria is the extent to which (with the benefit of a century's hindsight into advances in medical science) it has become clear that significant proportions of 'hysterics' were suffering from organic conditions which would now be readily diagnosable in other ways – such as temporal lobe epilepsy; organic brain damage; tuberculous meningitis; Tourette's syndrome; syphilis and multiple sclerosis (Webster 1995). As Shorter (1997) has outlined, the combined factors of suggestibility, social contagion, iatrogenesis and undiagnosed organic conditions largely explain the phenomenon of hysteria which so fascinated clinicians at the end of the nineteenth century.

The psychological notion of split or multiple consciousness is mostly associated with the work of Pierre Janet in France in the 1880s. Although Janet continues to be credited with being the primary influence in the development of understanding of dissociative disorders (and as a significant figure in the history of MPD), it is less well known that Janet himself came to view dual consciousness as a form of bipolar (manic depressive) disorder, and that he was expressly opposed to therapy which gave formal status to each 'part' as a separate entity (Merskey 1992, 1995; Mulhern 1994).

Interest in MPD began in America with Morton Prince's case study of Christine Beauchamp published in 1906 (Prince 1906, 1920). Prince described in detail his therapeutic interaction with his patient's three 'personalities'. However, while he noted her high level of suggestibility, he, like Freud, seemed oblivious of the impact of his actions and expectations on her responses (Kenny 1986). Following this case, recognition of MPD lay largely dormant throughout the world for several decades until the publication of *The Three Faces of Eve* (Thigpen and Cleckley 1954), which in turn became a popular film.[1] The case of 'Sybil' (Schreiber 1973) and other popular and influential films and publications followed two decades later, reiterating the same theme.[2] These two narratives provided a fashionable and influential (albeit stereotypical) template for expressions of personal distress and confusion, serving as the theoretical foundation for the new wave of multiple personality which has taken place in North America over the past 30 years. Readers are directed to Kenny (1986), Mulhern (1994), Pendergrast (1995) and Spanos (1996) for a more detailed review of the socio-anthropological issues relating to MPD.

One lesson which does not appear to have been fully learned from this history is that the combination of over-certain therapists and populations of unhappy vulnerable young women can lead to the promulgation of psychological theories and treatments which are resistant to theoretical scrutiny and clinical evaluation. A century after Charcot's circus, the same social process (which dates back centuries into demonology) whereby the afflicted and their healers combine with critical faculties suspended has recurred on a regular basis; and there is a great deal in the recent cultural construction of MPD which is directly evocative of the misguided treatments for hysteria of the last century.

Incidence of Multiple Personality Disorder

North America witnessed a large increase in reported incidence of MPD following intense media attention to 'Sybil' in the 1970s, the inclusion of MPD in the DSM III[3] in 1980, and the inauguration in 1984 of the annual International Conference on Multiple Personality/Dissociative States.[4] Notwithstanding professional discussion about MPD dating back for over a century, the overall reported incidence of this condition elsewhere in the world has consistently been extremely low. In fact there is little independent research which documents the existence of MPD on any scale outside of a specific therapeutic sub-culture predominantly in the USA and Canada.[5]

Commentators have noted that there were only about 200 cases in the world literature prior to 1980, and that between 1930 to 1960 only approximately two cases per decade were reported (Merskey 1995; Piper 1996). In contrast Putman *et al.* (1986) stated that more cases of MPD had been reported in the five year period to 1986 than in the past two centuries. Ross (1987) reported that 4.4 per cent of a sample of Canadian psychiatric inpatients, 5 per cent of Canadian college students, and one per cent of the general population were diagnosable as MPD. Merskey (1995) has strongly challenged the generalizability of such findings, arguing that they were a consequence of small numbers of MPD-orientated practitioners diagnosing huge numbers of cases.

Without high profile cultural attention and an active therapeutic subculture (which does not currently exist in the UK) the base rate for MPD appears to be very low. Research is needed to clarify whether MPD involves a naturally occurring rare phenomenon, or whether it exists unrecognized on a much greater scale. Few sceptics of MPD go so far as to claim that the condition does not naturally occur at all. Indeed it is impossible to prove that a condition does not exist. In North America, sceptics highlight the ratio of false positive to true positive diagnoses, concerned that the direction of error (and the magnitude of iatrogenic damage) lies significantly in favour of erroneous diagnoses of MPD. Lack of agreed valid diagnostic instruments and procedures makes this question a particularly difficult one to resolve. However, until there is substantial evidence in the UK of a population of false negatives (i.e. people who have been demonstrably and detrimentally affected by a failure to diagnose MPD) it is important that the professional community is vigilant about the potential wrongly to diagnose and treat clients for MPD.

Diagnosis of MPD

The current official diagnostic criteria for Multiple Personality Disorder are set out in the DSM IV (APA 1994) – the North American psychiatrists' bible. The DSM constitutes current diagnostic categories which are developed in professional committees through discussion, negotiation and compromise. As such they are subject to significant social and political influence (Mulhern 1997).[6] The diagnostic category of MPD was included in DSM III for the first time in 1980; and was substantially revised in 1987 (DSM III R). By 1994 (in the face of increasing professional scepticism) 'Multiple Personality Disorder' had been retitled with the somewhat less dramatic term 'Dissociative Identity Disorder' (DID). DSM IV highlights the contentious nature of the diagnosis:

> Controversy exists concerning the differential diagnosis between Dissociative Identity Disorder and a variety of other mental disorders . . .

Some clinicians believe that Dissociative Identity Disorder has been underdiagnosed . . . in contrast, others are concerned that Dissociative Identity Disorder may be overdiagnosed relative to other mental disorders based on media interest in the disorder and the suggestible nature of the individuals.

(APA 1994: 487)

Predictions are already being made, given the increase in malpractice suits in the USA against MPD therapists, that the condition will eventually be deleted from subsequent DSM editions (Kenny 1995).

DSM IV criteria for MPD/DID are:

A The presence of two or more distinct identities or personality states (each with its own relatively enduring pattern of perceiving, relating to, and thinking about the environment and self).
B At least two of these identities or personality states recurrently take control of the person's behaviour.[7]
C Inability to recall important personal information that is too extensive to be explained by ordinary forgetfulness.
D The disturbance is not due to the direct physiological effects of a substance (for example blackouts or chaotic behaviour during Alcohol Intoxication) or a general medical condition (for example complex partial seizures).

(APA 1994: 487)

By definition, MPD treatment should not be instigated for people who do not meet these criteria. In particular note the fourth criterion: potential organic explanations for symptoms must be excluded. This is especially important, as many reported MPD symptoms have some similarity with other more established conditions such as temporal lobe epilepsy, bipolar disorder, schizophrenia, acute anxiety, panic attacks, borderline personality disorder, antisocial personality disorder, somatization disorder and factitious disorder. Also, MPD is invariably a co-morbid condition – that is, it is usual for patients simultaneously to fulfil other DSM criteria as well as MPD (Piper 1996). This gives rise to the question as to which diagnosis should be given greater precedence in treatment responses. MPD proponents believe that MPD is the 'superordinate' diagnosis and that MPD treatments should take precedence over other treatments. They also consider that MPD is significantly underdiagnosed and that many people with intractable psychiatric problems (for example schizophrenic symptoms) are really undiagnosed MPD.

To support this, research is often cited which appears to suggest that MPD patients have been given inappropriate diagnoses and treatments on average for between seven and ten years before receiving their MPD diagnosis

(Kluft 1987; Coons *et al.* 1988; Kendall 1997). However, there is no convincing evidence that the MPD diagnoses which these patients received was the final diagnosis in their psychiatric careers, nor that MPD treatment had helped them. Consequently, sceptics consider that patients should first of all be treated in accordance with the more established diagnoses and that reinforcing attention to the MPD phenomena should be minimized: 'Multiple Personality Disorder is an iatrogenic behavioural syndrome, promoted by suggestion, social consequences, and group loyalties. It rests on ideas about the self that obscure reality, and it responds to standard treatments' (McHugh 1993).

A variety of screening instruments are used in North America which it is claimed detect undiscovered MPD in populations where this has not so far been a noticeable phenomenon.[8] There is significant disagreement, within the scientific community which is familiar with these instruments, about their validity and utility in accurately diagnosing MPD and successfully distinguishing it from other disorders (Piper 1996).

Multiple Personality Disorder treatment approaches

Over the last three decades, a new therapeutic sub-culture[9] committed to beliefs in widespread undiagnosed MPD has provided treatment for significant numbers of vulnerable (and often highly suggestible) clients desperate for understanding and solutions to their unhappiness. In their most damaging manifestation the beliefs of such therapists include combinations of assumptions:

- that extensive repressed memories of severe sexual abuse underlie presenting problems;
- that repressed memories of extensive ritualistic and satanic abuse (such as participation in sacrifices of babies, cannibalism, forced abortions and breeding of babies for slaughter) underlie presenting problems;
- that the hidden existence of numerous discrete dissociated identities ('alters') – of all ages, both sexes, including animals, is a consequence of severe child abuse;
- that MPD is a consequence of extensive mind-control programming by highly organized 'cults' of ritualistic abusers.[10]

Influential practitioners have asserted that one of the first principles and goals of MPD-oriented therapy is that clients must accept and believe that they have multiple personalities: 'stabilization involves the survivor's acceptance of their diagnosis and commitment to treatment. Diagnosis is in itself a crisis, and much work must be done to reframe DID as a creative survival tool (which it is) rather than a disease or stigma' (Turkus 1992).

The commonly reported style of such MPD treatment is based upon therapeutic encouragement for clients continually to produce 'alters', and to express cathartically 'recovered' memories of abuse. 'Alters' are dissociated identities with distinct personalities and differing life histories, which are amnesic of each others' existence and activities. In therapy 'alters' are invited by name to appear and to take control of the client's body; and therapists interact with each 'alter' in accordance with its self-proclaimed characteristics. Consequently therapists play on the floor with child 'alters'; baby-talk and bottle-feed infantile 'alters' – and presumably tickle the tummies of cat 'alters' and take dog 'alters' for walkies.

The dubious rationale is that all of the 'alters' must be uncovered and identified, and inducted into a therapeutic relationship on their own terms. Prominent 'alters' are enlisted to reach reticent 'alters'; and cooperative 'alters' act as co-therapists to cajole destructive 'alters'.[11] In addition, a 'host' is expected (and invariably appears) who has executive overview (but not total control) over this multifarious and chaotic internal community.[12] Once all 'alters' are uncovered and available for interaction with the therapist and each other (which apparently can be expected to take many years) the business of internal negotiation between 'alters' and their contradictory beliefs, expectations and needs can begin. The theory is that harmony between (tens, scores, or on occasions hundreds) of 'alters' will be brought about by the entire 'alter' system being explicitly mapped and facilitated into communication. This will promote a move toward gradual co-consciousness, increasing voluntary control over 'switching' (between alters); and an ultimate integration or fusion which is indicative of 'cure'.[13] Many MPD therapists (and the ISSD guidelines) casually assume that this will require between three to ten years of intensive psychotherapy – usually requiring two or three sessions per week (ISSD 1997).

These approaches are inherently regressive and disintegrative. As far as I know this is the only type of therapy which deliberately and systematically seeks to intensify and elaborate the symptoms which are seen as being the core of the disorder. Apparently, to make patients better, it is necessary first of all to make them significantly worse (Mulhern 1994; Merskey 1995; Robbins 1995; Piper 1996).

This approach to MPD (which is closely associated with beliefs in extensive undercover ritualistic abuse networks) became highly contagious in North America. It provided an attractive 'explains all' ideology; excitement from a sub-cultural development and application of 'special' knowledge; and was self-legitimizing via its resonance with anti child abuse agendas. It also offered the prospect of fascinating and highly imaginative work with long-term, highly dependent clients – whose extensive and expensive treatments (often in for-profit in-patient psychiatric facilities) were reimbursed by insurance companies on the basis that MPD was an 'authentic DSM I disorder'.[14]

Influenced by authoritative and charismatic MPD 'experts', newly converted therapists began to induct credulous clients into these belief systems. Like Charcot's and Freud's hysterics a century before, some clients accepted these suggestions and came to believe genuinely that they had multiple personalities. They responded with role-appropriate behaviour (acting out increasing varieties of alters), performances which were then enthusiastically reinforced (Bikel 1995; Hanson 1998).

Mulhern has noted that therapeutic movements which promote beliefs in the extensive prevalence of repressed memories of sexual abuse, ritualistic and satanistic abuse, MPD, and the widespread existence of sophisticated cult programming often have a defensive, somewhat paranoid, flavour which is impervious to theoretical incongruities and contradictory research (Mulhern 1994). At its strongest, the resulting iatrogenic process and impact is similar to inductions into cults – involving seductive (and sometimes coercive) combinations of:

- charismatic and authoritarian leader (therapist);
- heavily promoted expectancies of instant solutions/salvation from adoption of new belief system (MPD);
- reinterpretation of and separation from significant others (for example construing other family members as malevolent and severing contact);
- isolation from other sources of support and opinion;
- creation and reinforcement of emotional dependency;
- initiation, learning, and reinforcement of new ideology and expected behaviour (MPD symptoms) via group pressure (MPD group therapy).

This cult-like process of MPD-oriented therapy was harrowingly demonstrated by Ofra Bikel in the documentary *Divided Memories* (Bikel 1995). In the face of this material, it is difficult not to conclude that if there are organized cults at work on any scale in the child abuse arena, it is some MPD-oriented therapists themselves who wittingly or unwittingly constitute the cult – via induction of clients into MPD doctrine which includes the belief that their problems stem from another cult which is out to get them.

Concerns about these approaches are highlighted by the surprising paucity of research into MPD treatment. Despite the resurgence of the MPD field in North America over the past 30 years, there are no published independent treatment outcome follow-up studies; no published studies which compare different treatment approaches for people with an MPD diagnosis; and even a lack of convincing good outcome treatment case studies. By contrast, there is an accumulation of material which reinforces reservations about MPD therapy. This includes:

- research showing that high USA/Canada rates of MPD stem from small numbers of committed practitioners diagnosing large numbers of cases (Merskey 1995);

- reports of non-MPD orientated practitioners who work with casualties of MPD therapy (Robbins 1995);
- evidence that ritualistic abuse memories of some MPD patients are demonstrably false (Yeager and Lewis 1997);
- increasing number of settlements of malpractice claims in the USA/Canada – with many more in the pipeline (Bellock 1997; Grinfield 1997; Smith 1997; Nissimov 1998);
- vivid examples from depositions in malpractice claims about what MPD treatments can involve (Hanson 1998);
- examples from sceptical inquirers regarding the cult-like regimes of some MPD-oriented therapists (Bikel 1995; Pendergrast 1995);
- reports from US researchers regarding dynamics of life within Dissociative Disorder in-patient units. These include descriptions of the special status of MPD patients; competition among patients as to who could develop the most 'alters' and be 'Star patient'; and competition among therapists for status derived from having the patient with the most 'alters' (Lynn and Pintar 1997).

Some readers may feel that I have presented an exaggerated caricature of the MPD phenomenon and associated therapeutic approaches; and that this represents an unfair over-generalization from the reports of the 'wackier' elements within the field as a whole. I concede that I have been somewhat provocative and that there may be some grounds for such criticism. My intention, however, is to stress the need for therapists – and current and potential clients – to be aware that the fields of child abuse, psychology, counselling and psychotherapy can generate superficially plausible, contagious theories and therapies which can, and do, cause significant harm (Dale 1998).

Happily, most of the wackier MPD therapeutic beliefs and practices are restricted to the USA and Canada.[15] In the UK, MPD has an extremely low profile. For example, in a sample of the proceedings of the British Psychological Society in 1996/1997 MPD/DID was mentioned in only one out of more than 650 conference papers (BPS 1998). A few practitioners are attempting to generate professional discussion about the topic (Walker 1992; Mollon 1996); and this book will be a significant additional contribution.

I am concerned that discussion of MPD in the UK should not adopt and follow on from outdated and largely discredited North American models. The organization of therapists who work with MPD (the International Society for the Study of Dissociation – ISSD) is noticeably reticent about making explicit public statements regarding bad practice in the MPD field. This is surprising, as the current version (1997) of the ISSD *Guidelines for Treating Dissociative Identity Disorder* now strongly discourages many of the therapeutic practices which came to be associated with MPD in the 1980s and early 1990s.[16] The

1997 guidelines also take a strong position in favour of therapy focusing on maintaining and enhancing the daily functioning of clients – in direct contrast to previous expectations in the field that patients should expect to disintegrate as part of the 'treatment' process. These 1997 revisions are very welcome. However, they continue to reflect an unresolved tension and impasse in the MPD field as a whole between the influential cult programming/ritualistic-abuse wing (Noblitt and Perskin 1995) and other more cautious, scientifically grounded practitioners.

Notwithstanding the 1997 ISSD *Guidelines*, there is considerable evidence that many practitioners in the field continue to subscribe to the old treatment models. This is not helped by the refusal of ISSD to condemn publicly widely publicized accounts of bad practice. Without such statements, there is a risk that some therapists in the UK could continue to be guided by 1980s style MPD approaches, or even be newly converted to them, believing them still to be 'state of the art' practice in North America. There are hopeful signs that leading UK practitioners who work with MPD are taking a more cautious and tentative stance. Mollon's view, for example, is very different from the dominant North American models in that he believes that MPD is predominantly a disorder of believed-in pretence: 'A patient with MPD is a person pretending to have a multiple personality . . . the alter is a pretence, an illusion which is believed' (Mollon 1996: 127).

In contrast to stereotypical and prescriptive treatment approaches, he also argues that current knowledge about MPD, and how therapists should respond to it, remains very inadequate: 'I do not know how best to treat patients with severe dissociative disorders . . . the idea of a standardised therapy for patients with MPD/DID seems a contradiction in terms' (Mollon 1996: 140).

Understanding Liza's story

It is clear that at the time of writing her story Liza believes that she has MPD. I hope she is making good progress and that participating in this book will prove to be beneficial. There is a significant absence in the MPD literature of case studies with good outcomes on follow-up post therapy. I hope, for her sake, that Liza's case will ultimately prove to be an example of this.

Liza presents a great deal of material which provokes discussion about the nature of MPD; other potential explanations for her problems and distress; and alternative therapeutic approaches. There are a number of reasons to consider carefully whether the types of problems Liza describes are related to MPD or not and consequently whether MPD oriented therapy is necessarily the most appropriate way of responding to her continuing difficulties. Will it turn out to be the case (as in increasing numbers of examples reported in the USA and Canada) that clients such as Liza will make most progress when they have freed themselves from a transient MPD belief system and a therapy which reinforces this?

In her account Liza makes reference to an extensive range of symptoms and problems including:

- high levels of anxiety and panic attacks;
- a serious alcohol problem;
- eating problems;
- self-mutilating behaviour;
- a reported history of epilepsy;
- irrational thoughts and beliefs (re. the fire);
- a history of destructive relationships;
- problems in parenting her children (rages and screaming at them);
- 'mental breakdown' when her friend Jason died;
- experiences of depersonalization and derealization;
- a sense of identity confusion;
- withdrawal from psychotropic medication;
- constant memories of chronic and multiple childhood abuse;
- the 'recovery' of memories of childhood abuse;
- experience of multiple personalities.

Any medical investigation (including psychiatry) begins with a check for the simplest and most common explanations for reported problems, and systematically excludes these before actively exploring the possibility of more complex, ominous, and rare underlying conditions. Such an approach, in my view, is also the most effective principle to follow in general counselling and psychotherapy practice when people present with specific symptoms and problems. It makes sense to the client, respects their phenomenology, and is orientated towards perceptions of Self as normal and potentially healthy, while assuming that therapeutic intervention is likely to be fairly brief unless the need is proved to be otherwise.

The notion of Multiple Personality Disorder is one possible way of understanding Liza's combination of severe and disabling difficulties. However, there are other more common potential explanations which should be considered before treatment commences in response to a less likely condition. Therapists who are committed to the notion of extensive undiagnosed MPD underlying a wide range of presenting problems (such as those listed above) tend to short-cut this process. They focus prematurely and single-mindedly on the MPD hypothesis without having considered (and provided appropriate treatments for) other diagnoses which are more common – albeit less spectacular and intriguing.

There are other reasons to be cautious about a diagnosis of MPD on the basis of the information presented. As I have discussed earlier, diagnoses relate to criteria outlined in the DSM IV (APA 1994), and, in particular, criterion 'D' does not appear to be clearly met in Liza's case: 'The disturbance is not due to the direct physiological effects of a substance (for example blackouts or chaotic behaviour during Alcohol Intoxication) or a general medical condition (for example complex partial seizures)' (APA 1994: 487).

In fact, Liza's story highlights both of these examples: a significant history of excessive alcohol consumption (a bottle of whisky a day); and previous diagnosis and treatment for epilepsy. A diagnosis of MPD should not be made (and MPD focused treatment not initiated) until and unless there is firm medical/psychiatric evidence that a combination of reactions relating to epilepsy, alcohol and medication has been excluded as contributing to the phenomena which are currently being construed as MPD.

It would also be important to explore carefully suggestive influences on the development of MPD beliefs/experiences and potential secondary gains from being considered to have this condition. In Liza's case, the diagnosis of MPD is confounded by her first awareness of MPD stemming from reading a book on the subject; and from participating in a group for survivors of sexual abuse during which 'the personalities started to emerge more clearly'. Both of these social influences have high levels of suggestible effect in certain vulnerable individuals (Lindsay and Read 1995; Lynn and Pintar 1997). Also, in general, it is well known that dissociative individuals are highly suggestible (Lynn *et al.* 1988).

Many of Liza's reported problems are commonly associated with histories of chronic childhood abuse. The background Liza has always been aware of (chronic multiple abuse, neglect and family disturbance) is more than sufficient to account for many of her cognitive, emotional, self-esteem and relationship difficulties. There is need for particular caution regarding interpretation of Liza's additional 'recovered' memories of childhood abuse. It is important that she understands that such 'recovered' memories may be essentially accurate, a mixture of accurate and imagined, or completely untrue.[17] Also, that there is no way of knowing from the experience of 'remembering' itself (for example 'flashbacks', vividness, and emotional intensity of recall) how accurate these memories are (Dale and Allen 1998). This is often fundamentally misunderstood by people who were abused as children – and by many therapists.

Liza's account reads as though she has assimilated some of these misconceptions about child abuse memory processes. This would not be surprising, as much of the abuse 'survivor' literature of the 1980s and early 1990s presented a picture of abuse memories which is now known to be fundamentally flawed (Read and Lindsay 1997). Many therapists also assimilated such misunderstandings and passed them on to clients (Yapko 1993; Poole *et al.* 1995). Consequently, styles of therapy developed in which therapists 'validated' all memories as being literally accurate. Today, it is increasingly accepted that (in the absence of external corroboration) therapists cannot interpret whether 'recovered' memories of abuse are true or not. Rather than providing routine 'validation', therapy should help develop clients' reality-testing abilities and, often, to recognize that a state of uncertainty about the accuracy of certain memories may need to be accepted. Liza needs to be aware of this.

Provision of MPD-oriented treatment for vulnerable, confused and desperately unhappy people can have an iatrogenic effect – whereby the 'treatment' induces clients to display the symptoms and behaviours expected by their therapists. This reflects either a factitious response (the client is aware of play-acting to please the therapist) or a believed-in pretence as described by Mollon (1996). I am not suggesting that Liza's therapist has been operating in the extreme iatrogenic way described in some of the North American literature. However, these influences can have more subtle manifestations which affect therapists' beliefs and expectations, and clients' responses to these. Consequently, as part of a continual assessment of Liza's difficulties and therapeutic needs, it would be important to review carefully the helpful and unhelpful impact of her previous therapeutic experiences – as well her expectations as to what further therapy can achieve.

The most important focus for a client such as Liza (particularly bearing in mind that she is also the parent of young children) is to concentrate on gaining control over her current disabling symptoms. Clearly many efforts have already been made in this direction without marked success. However, lack of success from the use of established techniques to stabilize these types of disturbances is not, in itself, reason to adopt alternative and controversial approaches. For a client who has severe problems in dealing with everyday life, to utilize destabilizing techniques (such as identifying and regressively acting out 'alters' and working to excavate further 'repressed' memories of childhood abuse) is particularly inappropriate and potentially damaging.

Instead, a sustained predominantly cognitive-behavioural approach is indicated for this important stabilization phase of therapy (Jehu 1988; Briere 1997; Courtois 1997). When progress in this area has been consolidated (and development of increased maturity through the passage of time can be an important factor), attention can then turn to problems associated with confused sense of self and identity, and difficulties in relationships as reported by Liza. In this way the focus shifts towards competence and future aspirations, rather than remaining stuck in past-oriented abuse-focused therapy, or in negative present-oriented self-reinforcing rumination on MPD-type phenomena.

Not having met Liza, I cannot say that my suggestions will be the right ones for her. I do not know how committed Liza is to the notion that she has multiple personalities; nor whether she currently considers this to be a disorder (in search of effective treatment) or a way of being (in need of consistent expression and family and social acceptance). In reflecting upon this, it is important that Liza (and other clients in similar situations) is aware of the controversies surrounding MPD and – as I have outlined in this chapter – knows that many MPD treatment approaches anchor clients to MPD belief systems within which their problems do not improve.

In view of the lack of independent research to provide support for the efficacy of MPD-oriented therapy, therapists have an ethical duty to warn clients and potential clients that knowledge about MPD and associated therapy remains at an experimental stage. As part of the process of obtaining informed consent for therapy, clients should be informed of this, and given information about the controversial nature of the diagnosis, the associated treatment techniques, and the accumulating reports of harmful outcomes of MPD treatment. Providing such information to facilitate fully informed consent must be understood as a required standard of care.

On this basis, MPD-oriented therapists who are committed to the 1997 ISSD guidelines can join forces with sceptics to warn potential clients to steer well clear of cavalier therapists who remain fascinated by, and committed to, the culture of 1970s and 1980s North American MPD ideology and practice. I hope that this book as a whole will reinforce my call for adults who were abused as children to take great care in this area.

Notes

1 In contrast to the current doctrine that severe childhood abuse underlies MPD, 'Eve' has always maintained that she was not abused as a child. The psychiatrists who presented her case, Thigpen and Cleckley, maintained that MPD was an extremely rare condition. They reported that in 30 years' practice post 'Eve' they were consulted about hundreds of patients who were thought to have MPD. In their view, all of these (bar one) were false positive diagnoses (Thigpen and Cleckley 1984).

2 Controversy continues about the case of 'Sybil'. The case study was not subject to the normal academic scrutiny which is involved in journal publication (Mulhern 1994). Instead the published account was written by a journalist. A psychiatrist who also examined 'Sybil' maintains that the MPD diagnosis was artificial (Merskey 1995).

3 *Diagnostic and Statistical Manual of Mental Disorders* (APA 1994).

4 The precursor of the International Society for the Study of Dissociation (ISSD).

5 There are reports of MPD in Holland (Boon and Draijer 1993).

6 Two examples of this are the original inclusion – and subsequent deletion – of homosexuality as a formal psychiatric condition. Similarly, 'Posttraumatic Stress Disorder' was included in 1980 following extensive lobbying by Vietnam war veterans for a non-stigmatizing diagnosis to the sequelae of combat.

7 It is interesting that this criterion is watered down from the DSM III R version in the 1987 version, which requires the identities or personality states to take full control of the person's behaviour.

8 One of these is the Dissociative Experiences Scale (DES), which is heavily weighted in favour of assuming the presence of severe dissociative experiences.

9 Almost entirely confined to the USA and Canada.

10 One well-known MPD authority believes that the CIA is involved in the creation of MPD via mind control programming. Others claim that experiences of abductions

Multiple Personality Disorder: a sceptical perspective   **53**

by aliens are implanted in MPD people by satanic cult leaders to conceal and per-
petuate extensive ritual abuse activities.

11 In June 1998 a US TV documentary highlighted the case of a client who killed his
therapist, then claimed that one of his 'alters' was the killer.

12 It is interesting that this central (and stereotypical) role of host – upon which so
much of MPD therapeutic practice depends – is not mentioned at all in the DSM IV
definition and description of MPD.

13 With the MPD sub-culture the notion of fusion is controversial. One view resists
the goal of fusion, proclaiming that MPD is a valuable alternative state of being.

14 Following a spate of malpractice suits brought by ex MPD patients, insurance companies in the USA have become much less willing to authorize long-term MPD
treatments. Many specialist 'Dissociative Disorders' treatment units have closed in
recent years. Many more claims for damages for malpractice are pending, including
a criminal prosecution of two well-known MPD authorities for insurance fraud
related to MPD in-patient treatments.

15 Readers with Internet access might find it interesting to search out the discussion
group alt.support.dissociation to get a flavour of MPD culture – including the frequent protests of dissatisfied MPD therapy clients.

16 Such as: exorcism; use of hypnosis and sodium amytal for diagnosis; viewing treatment as a process of memory excavation; routine belief in all memories; viewing
dissociated aspects of the personality as if they are separate people; routine use of
marathon sessions and multiple sessions every week; and presenting patients at
conferences and on TV.

17 This is also the official position of the ISSD 1997 guidelines.

References

American Psychiatric Association (APA) (1980) *Diagnostic and Statistical Manual of
Mental Disorders* (DSM III) USA: APA.
American Psychiatric Association (APA) (1987) *Diagnostic and Statistical Manual of
Mental Disorders* (DSM III R) USA: APA.
American Psychiatric Association (APA) (1994) *Diagnostic and Statistical Manual of
Mental Disorders* (DSM IV) USA: APA.
Bellock, P. (1997) 'Memory' therapy leads to a law suit and big settlement, *New York
Times*, 6 November.
Bikel, O. (1995) *Divided Memories*. USA: Frontline TV Documentary.
Boon, S., and Draijer, N. (1993) Multiple personality disorder in the Netherlands:
a clinical investigation of 71 patients, *American Journal of Psychiatry*, 150:
489–94.
Briere, J. (1997) An integrated approach to treating adults abused as children with spe-
cific reference to self-reported recovered memories, in J. D. Read and D. S. Lind-
say (eds) *Recollections of Trauma: Scientific Research and Clinical Practice*. New
York: Plenum.
British Psychological Society (BPS) (1998) *Proceedings of the British Psychological Society*,
6(1): 1–77.
Coons, P., Bowman, E. and Millstein, V. (1988) Multiple personality disorder: a clinical
investigation of 50 cases, *Journal of Nervous and Mental Disease*, 176: 519–27.
Courtois, C. A. (1997) Informed clinical practice and the standard of care: proposed
guidelines for treatment of adults who report delayed memories of childhood
trauma, in J. D. Read and D. S. Lindsay (eds) *Recollections of Trauma: Scientific
Research and Clinical Practice*. New York: Plenum.

Crews, F. C. (1998) *Unauthorized Freud: Doubters Confront a Legend*. New York: Viking.
Dale, P. (1998) *Adults Abused as Children: Experiences of Counselling and Psychotherapy*. London: Sage.
Dale, P. and Allen, J. (1998) On memories of childhood abuse: a phenomenological study, *Child Abuse and Neglect*, 22(8) 799–812.
Dale, P. and Fellows, R. (1999) Independent child protection assessments: incorporating a therapeutic focus from an integrated service context, *Child Abuse Review*, 8: 4–14.
Dale, P., Allen, J. and Measor, L. (1998) Counselling adults who were abused as children: Clients' perceptions of efficacy, client–counsellor communication and dissatisfaction, *British Journal of Guidance and Counselling*, 26(2): 141–57.
Grinfield, M. J. (1997) Psychiatrists liable for millions in civil suits, *Psychiatric Times*, December.
Hacking, I. (1995) *Rewriting the Soul: Multiple Personality and the Sciences of Memory*. Princeton, NJ: Princeton University Press.
Hanson, C. (1998) Dangerous therapy, *Chicago Magazine*, May.
International Society for the Study of Dissociation (ISSD) (1997) *Guidelines for Treating Dissociative Identity Disorder (Multiple Personality Disorder) in Adults*. Skokie, IL: ISSD.
Jehu, D. (1988) *Beyond Sexual Abuse: Therapy with Women Who Were Childhood Victims*. Chichester: Wiley.
Kendall, J. C. (1997) Advances in diagnosing and treating dissociative disorders, *Treating Abuse Today*, 2: 17–24.
Kenny, M. G. (1986) *The Passion of Ansel Bourne: Multiple Personality in American Culture*. Washington, DC: Smithsonian Press.
Kenny, M. G. (1995) The recovered memory controversy: an anthropologist's view, *The Journal of Psychiatry and Law*, Fall: 437–60.
Kluft, R. (1987) Making the diagnosis of multiple personality disorder, in F. Flach (ed.) *Diagnostics and Psychopathology*. New York: Norton.
Lindsay, D. S. and Read, J. D. (1995) 'Memory work' and recovered memories of childhood sexual abuse: scientific evidence and public, professional, and personal issues, *Psychology, Public Policy, and Law*, 1(4): 846–908.
Lynn, S. J. and Pintar, J. (1997) The social construction of multiple personality disorder, in J. D. Read and D. S. Lindsay (eds) *Recollections of Trauma: Scientific Research and Clinical Practice*. New York: Plenum.
Lynn, S. J., Rhue, J. and Green, J. (1988) Multiple personality and fantasy proneness: is there an association or dissociation? *British Journal of Experimental and Clinical Hypnosis*, 5: 138–42.
Masson, J. (1984) *The Assault on Truth: Freud's Suppression of the Seduction Theory*. New York: HarperPerennial.
McHugh, P. R. (1993) Multiple personality disorder, *Harvard Mental Health Newsletter*, 10: 4–6.
Merskey, H. (1992) The manufacture of personalities: the production of multiple personality disorder, *British Journal of Psychiatry*, 166: 327–40.
Merskey, H. (1995) Multiple personality disorder and false memory syndrome, *British Journal of Psychiatry*, 166: 281–3.
Mollon, P. (1996) *Multiple Selves, Multiple Voices: Working with Trauma, Violation and Dissociation*. Chichester: Wiley.
Mulhern, S. (1994) Satanism, ritual abuse, and multiple personality disorder: a sociohistorical perspective, *International Journal of Clinical and Experimental Hypnosis*, 42: 265–88.
Mulhern, S. (1997) Commentary on the logical status of case histories, in J. D. Read and

D. S. Lindsay (eds) *Recollections of Trauma: Scientific Research and Clinical Practice.* New York: Plenum.

Nissimov, R. (1998) Woman sues over false memories, *Houston Chronicle*, 20 April.

Noblitt, R. and Perskin, P. (1995) *Cult and Ritual Abuse: Its History, Anthropology, and Recent Discovery in Contemporary America.* Westport, CT: Praegar Publishers.

Pendergrast, M. (1995) *Victims of Memory: Sex Abuse Accusations and Shattered Lives.* Vermont: Upper Access, Inc.

Piper, A., Jr (1996) *Hoax and Reality: The Bizarre World of Multiple Personality Disorder.* New Jersey: Jason Aronson.

Poole, D. A., Lindsay, D. S., Memon, A. and Bull, R. (1995) Psychotherapy and the recovery of memories of childhood sexual abuse: U.S. and British practitioners' opinions, practices, and experiences, *Journal of Consulting and Clinical Psychology*, 63(3): 426–37.

Prince, M. (1906) *The Dissociation of a Personality.* New York: Longmans, Green.

Prince, M. (1920) Miss Beauchamp: the theory of the psychogenesis of multiple personality, *Journal of Abnormal Psychology*, 15: 67–135.

Putman, F. W., Post, R. M. and Guroff, J. J. (1986) One hundred cases of multiple personality disorder, *Journal of Clinical Psychiatry*, 47: 285–93.

Read, J. D. and Lindsay, D. S. (eds) (1997) *Recollections of Trauma: Scientific Research and Clinical Practice.* New York: Plenum.

Robbins, S. P. (1995) Cults, in *Encyclopedia of Social Work* (19th edn, vol. 1, pp. 667–76). Washington, DC: NASW Press.

Ross, C. A. (1987) Inpatient treatment of multiple personality disorder, *Canadian Journal of Psychiatry*, 32: 776–81.

Rowan, J. (1990) *Subpersonalities: The People Inside Us.* Routledge: London.

Schreiber F. R. (1973) *Sybil.* New York: Warner.

Shorter, E. (1997) *A History of Psychiatry: From the Era of the Asylum to the Age of Prozac.* New York: Wiley.

Smith, M. (1997) Jury awards $5.8 million in satanic memories case, *Houston Chronicle*, 15 August.

Spanos, N. P. (1996) *Multiple Identities and False Memories.* Washington, DC: American Psychological Association.

Thigpen, C. H. and Cleckley, H. M. (1954) A case of multiple personality, *Journal of Abnormal and Social Psychology*, 39: 135–51.

Thigpen, C. H. and Cleckley, H. M. (1984) On the incidence of multiple personality disorder: a brief communication, *International Journal of Clinical and Experimental Hypnosis*, 32(2): 63–6.

Thornton, E. M. (1984) *The Freudian Fallacy: An Alternative View of Freudian Theory.* Garden City, NY: Dial Press.

Turkus, J. A. (1992) The spectrum of dissociative disorders: an overview of diagnosis and treatment, in *Moving Forward*, Arlington: USA

Walker, M. (1992) *Surviving Secrets.* Buckingham: Open University Press.

Webster, R. (1995) *Why Freud Was Wrong: Sin, Science and Psychoanalysis.* London: HarperCollins.

Yapko, M. (1993) Suggestibility and repressed memories of abuse: a survey of psychotherapists' beliefs, *American Journal of Clinical Hypnosis*, 36(3): 163–71.

Yeager, C. A. and Lewis, D. O. (1997) False memories of cult abuse, *American Journal of Psychiatry*, 154(3): 435.

Chapter 4

Multiple selves, multiple voices, multiple transferences

Phil Mollon

Introduction

I cannot locate the origin of my interest in multiple personality/dissociative identity in either of my two background professional disciplines of clinical psychology and psychoanalytic psychotherapy. Although the study of multiple personality has a long history, as Cohen (1996) points out, it was not, until recently, given much thought by practitioners within the mainstream mental health traditions. In the mid 1980s I did hear someone refer to the fact that they were working with some patients with multiple personalities – and although I may have feigned polite interest, this seemed sufficiently obscure, both clinically and conceptually, to be of little concern. Moreover, my interest in childhood sexual abuse was also, at that time, minimal. While the notion of *fantasies* of incest was familiar enough, the Oedipus complex being an everyday focus of psychoanalytic work, the idea of actual sexual activity between a parent and child seemed obscure and unlikely. During my earlier professional practice, from 1974, and even during my training in psychotherapy at the Tavistock Clinic in the early 1980s, I did not knowingly encounter any patient who had been sexually abused in childhood *and I did not know anyone else who had.*

This position changed when I later began work in a general psychiatric setting. There I was not infrequently asked to see patients who were both very disturbed and very puzzling, and who strained existing diagnostic frameworks. These patients would allude to very severe interpersonal trauma in childhood, but would become extremely agitated if they attempted to talk about it. They would show shifting and radically different states of mind at different times. In some states they would be overwhelmed with primitive affect. The only relevant diagnostic category that I was aware of was 'borderline personality disorder', a psychoanalytic concept popularized by Kernberg in the 1970s. Kernberg (1975) did not link this diagnosis with child-hood trauma, but by 1987 some theorists were beginning to propose that borderline personality disorder was a kind of complex long-term post-traumatic stress disorder (Herman and van der Kolk 1987). However, descrip-tions of borderline personality did not normally include accounts of internal voices, which the patients I was seeing often indicated. Actually such voices were revealed hesitantly and with much anxiety; sometimes they seemed to form mafia-like structures (similar to descriptions by Rosenfeld 1971) which aimed to control and secretly dominate the personality. These voices would often not take kindly to being discovered by the therapist and would punish the patient for revealing their existence; for example, they might say that they would make the patient cut herself or take an overdose – and sometimes would succeed in doing so. Although Rosenfeld had, within the psychoana-lytic tradition, described malevolent organizations of internal figures, he had not portrayed their phenomenology as including internal voices; nor had he pointed to severe and repeated trauma as a significant causative factor, attributing the internal 'mafia' instead to the death instinct, a Freudian notion which had been taken up with enthusiasm by those analysts influ-enced by Melanie Klein. While the experience of hallucinatory voices might suggest a diagnosis of schizophrenia, these patients did not show other fea-tures one would expect in schizophrenia, such as thought disorder, delu-sions, bizarre ideas and blunting of affect.

Thus these patients did not fit the usual diagnostic frameworks of British psychiatry and psychoanalysis. However, I began to recognize the clinical phenomena I was encountering when I came upon the studies of trauma which had developed in the 1980s. Post-traumatic stress disorder was not well understood before this; Mardi Horowitz's landmark book *Stress Response Syndromes* was published in 1978 and was distinctly novel at the time. By 1987, some were beginning to theorize that borderline personality disorder was a kind of complex and characterologically structured form of post-traumatic stress disorder, with origins in repeated childhood interper-sonal trauma (Herman and van der Kolk 1987). The study of trauma returned more fully to psychoanalysis with a book published in 1988 by Ulman and Brothers called *The Shattered Self – A Psychoanalytic Study of Trauma*. In 1989, two books appeared which presented the phenomena of multiple personality disorder in considerable detail and postulated that its origins lay in severe and repeated childhood abuse (Putman 1989; Ross 1989). These books described the clinical phenomena I was encountering.

However, the emerging literature on MPD was not psychoanalytic, tending to draw on cognitive-behavioural frameworks and to make use of hypnosis in treatment. Attention to psychoanalytic phenomena, such as transference and unconscious communication, including the unconscious use of metaphor, was missing. Moreover, all the literature was from the USA.

I decided it was time to write my own book on the subject, partly in order to facilitate my own thinking and to help me to integrate this material with psychoanalysis, which I still regard as my 'home' discipline (Mollon 1996). One particular point needed addressing. The trauma literature frequently referred to the defence of dissociation. This did not appear in psychoanalytic writings, with odd exceptions such as Fairbairn, even though psychoanalysis was essentially concerned with mental defences. Part of the reason may lie in the origins of psychoanalysis a hundred years ago, when Freud's paradigm of conflict and repression was in ideological conflict with Janet's theory of trauma and dissociation (Mollon 1996). The defences described within psychoanalytic literature have tended to apply to intrapsychic danger rather than to external threat and exogenous trauma. This situation in now changing. Recently I attended a conference on psychoanalytic research, with particular reference to trauma and aggression. The concept of dissociation cropped up very frequently in the discussion. One eminent professor of psychoanalysis commented that when faced with danger human beings have three options: to fight, take flight, or dissociate. It seems that psychoanalysis may now be ready to embrace a concept which it once rejected.

The prevalence of dissociative disorders: overt and covert/latent DID

How widespread is DID? Estimates vary widely. Since clinicians vary considerably in their propensity to diagnose DID, a true rate is difficult to ascertain. The position is complicated further because there is a wide spectrum of dissociative states, the full DID with several elaborated alters being only one extreme form of dissociative disorder. During the last ten years I have seen only six cases of full DID. This is in the context of assessing two or three new patients each week – a frequency of less than 5 in 1000 psychiatric patients. All but one of these DID cases were referred by psychiatrists; all had significant psychiatric histories. On the other hand I have seen a large number of patients with some more limited dissociative tendency, such as internal hallucinatory voices, often also associated with borderline personality disorder, and in every case reporting a history of childhood abuse. These lesser forms of dissociative disorder could often fall into the DSM IV category of Dissociative Disorder Not Otherwise Specified (DDNOS).

I have also encountered what could be termed latent DID. For example, Mrs D had for some years managed not to think about childhood experiences of abuse. This not thinking became more difficult when she had her own children. In an effort to find help with these now intrusive and disturbing recollections of childhood, she began work with a client centred counsellor. The counsellor employed a standard non-directive technique and certainly did not request or encourage a focus on childhood trauma; moreover, the counsellor was not familiar with DID. Mrs D had never spoken about her childhood abuse before and found some relief, mixed with considerable anxiety, in talking about it to the counsellor. However, the more she talked the more she seemed to remember – and the more she remembered the more overwhelmed she became. She began to dissociate into frightened child states of mind during counselling sessions and often experienced difficulty in returning to an adult state. This increasing regression and dissociation became particularly difficult for her when she found herself in child states of mind while at home with responsibility for her own children. Far from being helped and stabilized by the counselling she became less and less able to cope, dissociating rapidly and frequently becoming disoriented, anxious and confused, and losing memory for periods of time. She decided to stop the counselling and found that this enabled her to stabilize again. However, she still felt profoundly troubled by intrusive memories of childhood abuse. Did the dissociative alters exist before the counselling? My impression is that Mrs D had a latent dissociative disorder, with child alters containing the various experiences of abuse, and that the process of talking to one who would listen allowed this to become a manifest disorder. This example illustrates a crucial point – that uncovering is not always helpful. Some patients can be destabilized simply by the process of talking and being listened to.

Since writing *Multiple Selves*, I have been consulted by a number of psychotherapists who have been startled to discover their patient's elaborate dissociative aspects only some time after beginning therapy. Dissociation is, in its nature, hidden. Patients often do not openly reveal their multiplicity, fearing disbelief, ridicule or misdiagnosis as schizophrenic. A person with an elaborate dissociative disorder may present a deceptively healthy personality, such that the therapist initially thinks they have an only moderately troubled neurotic patient. It may be months or years later when the patient suddenly turns up in a totally different personality state, creating bewilderment and alarm in the therapist – but by then the psychotherapeutic voyage is well under way and it is too late to turn back.

The origin and function of DID – trauma in a corrupt environment

Most contemporary theorists consider that DID has its roots in severe and repeated childhood trauma, from which there is no escape other than dissociation. If one cannot successfully fight against a threatening or aggressive figure nor run away, then the only alternative is to escape internally through dissociation. Thus Liza describes memories of physical, sexual and emotional abuse. She reports being raped at the age of 4. She also refers to an awareness of her father's sexual desire for her, expressed by staring at her as well as groping her in the shower. She reports a further extreme trauma in the form of being locked in the garage at night when she was a 2-year-old baby. Probably Liza learned to detach herself from unbearable experiences, and this would have been combined with the use of imagination and pretence in order to arrive at a protective belief that someone other than herself was being abused. In this way the creation of alter personalities would have begun.

Three different levels and forms of dissociation may be distinguished, all being responses to trauma (van der Kolk *et al.* 1996). Primary dissociation is the somatosensory fragmentation which occurs immediately in response to severe trauma, including war trauma; secondary dissociation is the separation between an experiencing and an observing self, resulting in the phenomena of depersonalization and derealization; tertiary dissociation, evolving in response to repeated interpersonal trauma over a period of time, is the elaboration of distinct personality states, which may have individual names, affects, memories and styles of cognition.

Several authors consider that DID is essentially based on pretence (employed against overwhelming trauma). Thus Kluft (1994: 16) comments:

> On a clinical and descriptive level, MPD is, intrinsically, no more than a brutalised child's whimpering in the night and wishing with desparate earnestness that he or she were someone else, somewhere else, and that what had befallen him or her had befallen someone else. Most parsimoniously put, MPD appears to be a dissociative condition of childhood onset . . .

and Ross (1989: 55) remarks:

> MPD is a little girl imagining that the abuse is happening to someone else . . . The imagining is so intense, subjectively compelling, and adaptive, that the abused child experiences dissociated aspects of herself as other people . . .

Indeed one could say that a patient with a multiple personality is a person *pretending* to have a multiple personality – but the pretence has structured the personality development from early childhood. The personality is built around pretence and spontaneous self-hypnosis.

However, it should not be assumed that the dissociation is an essentially intrapsychic phenomenon, existing only in the mind of the one who is abused. The victim's dissociation mirrors the distortions, inconsistencies, secrets and compartmentalizations in the environment. Dissociation exists within a dissociative relationship. Studies of offenders (Wyre 1987; Salter 1995) reveal that sexual abuse of children takes place often in a context of very extensive strategic planning over a period of time. Part of the aim of this is to achieve profound control over what the child feels and thinks, as well as over his or her behaviour: this fact becomes apparent only through the sort of detailed interviews with offenders which sex crime consultant Ray Wyre has carried out. The offender will endeavour to ensure that the child cannot speak about the abuse and perhaps not even think about it. This may be done through creating in the child a sense of guilt, shame and responsibility for the sexual activity, as well as inducing confusion. Distorted views may be communicated which conflict with the child's natural intuition that what is being done is not benign; for example, the child may be told that the abuse is an expression of love. The abuser may behave in quite different and emotionally incompatible ways at different times, without any reference between one behavioural state and another; for example, an abuser may appear kind and considerate in one situation but abusive and threatening at another time. The child may specifically be told that he/she must not speak about the abuse to others within the family or outside. All these processes make normal awareness, thought, association of ideas, memory and communication extremely compromised. For many who were sexually abused in childhood, becoming able to speak at all about the abuse is a remarkable achievement.

The point about this is that it is not trauma *per se* which leads to dissociation and disturbance of memory and awareness, but abusive trauma in the context of a corrupt relationship. This is the core of Jennifer Freyd's (1996) theory of 'betrayal trauma', that awareness of abuse may conflict with a more primary need for survival in the context of a relationship with a primary care giver. She found support for her theory by reanalysing the data from some of the studies of amnesia for childhood sexual abuse; memory disturbance was associated with a close relationship with the abuser. Abuse by a stranger does not usually lead to memory disturbance.

In her account, Liza gives hints of some of the ways in which her childhood interpersonal environment was grossly abnormal, but as she indicates, she did not at the time realize that it was abnormal: 'I thought all dads were the same.' She was profoundly confused and frightened: 'The emotional abuse made everything so unpredictable you never knew where you stand. So you don't trust anybody; you don't know what's right and wrong . . . it was like godliness in the daytime and evil at night.' She describes an overwhelming and intrusive awareness of her father's sexual desire for her, resulting in pervasive shame and wish to hide: 'I can't bear eye contact and I know that's because my father always stared at me. I suppose I spent most of my childhood looking at the floor.' It is clear from Liza's account that a bizarre quality pervaded her father's responses to her, peculiar sexual content intruding very frequently: 'one of the personalities came home in a rage about something and she smashed the bedroom up and I remember dad sitting in the living room shouting "she's only smashing it up because she's knobbing him. And she don't like it."'

Part of what Liza describes is an extreme corruption and aberration of power: 'on the one hand as a child I'm being took to confession when I haven't done anything wrong, and there you've got dad doing exactly what he wants when he wants and nobody says anything, and that doesn't matter because that's dad.' This is a family in which there is no law. Perhaps the fundamental 'law' is the incest taboo, the prohibition which determines with whom the father can and cannot have sex. Liza's father's free violation of this law means that nothing is sacred and there is no knowing what he might do. No doubt Liza felt that ultimately she could be killed by her father.

Liza describes collusion by her mother who turned a blind eye to the father's abuse: 'he puts his hand up my nightie and starts rubbing my bum and I remember standing there feeling horrible and frozen and my mum would just look at me and look away, and I'd be thinking, mum, will you tell him to stop but she just turns away'. This capacity on the part of a mother to turn away from awareness of the abuse by the father who dominates the household is described vividly, in relation to the case of the mass murderer Fred West, by Brian Masters (1997) in his book *She Must Have Known*. West was a law unto himself, dominating his family and sexually abusing them in every conceivable way.

In such circumstances, where there is felt to be real danger every day, with no external escape from the danger, survival requires complex mental contortions in an effort to adapt to a highly abnormal environment. Blocking of normal thinking and compartmentalization of experience may be combined with the use of imagination in order to create an internal group – providing 'safety in numbers' and adaptively developing a variety of responses and personality styles to maximize survival in a hostile environment. The capacity to dissociate prevents the whole of the personality being overwhelmed with the violation. To use a slightly odd (but at the time of writing, topical) analogy, the *Titanic* would not have sunk after its violation by the iceberg if it had had the capacity to seal off its areas of injury and prevent leakage into its whole space; if it had been able to do so, the majority of the happy revellers could have continued their activities blissfully unaware of the damage. *Titanic* sank because it was assumed to have more capacity for dissociation than it did in fact have.

Is a multiple personality an iatrogenic creation?

A common criticism of the diagnostic concept of multiple personality/dissociative identity disorder is the proposition that it is an artificial product of a therapeutic approach which encourages this form of presentation – i.e. that it is iatrogenic. It is argued that this is why only a relatively few clinicians diagnose DID and why these few may diagnose it frequently. A combination of a particularly suggestible patient and a persuasive therapist who believes in DID is said to result in the presentation of alter personalities. Notable protagonists of this point of view are Aldrige-Morris (1989) and Spanos (1996), although many others appear to subscribe to this view. A particularly obscure version of this argument is given by the philosopher, Hacking (1995). All these texts have a distinctly polemical tone.

I have no doubt that, in its extreme form, the explanation in terms of iatrogenesis is wrong. Just recently I was referred a patient, with a background of abuse, who told me that she had for as long as she could remember experienced herself as containing a variety of personalities with different names. She had felt most reluctant to reveal this to the psychiatrist who referred her to me, fearing that she would be regarded as mad, or simply not believed. I enquired whether she had read about MPD or DID or seen any TV programmes, or talked to other patients about these diagnoses. She had never even heard of the concept! She appeared most surprised and relieved that I seemed to understand and be familiar with some of what she told me. Having discussed a little of her experience of herself she expressed a mixture of curiosity and great anxiety as to what therapy might entail.

Those patients I have seen whom I would consider unequivocally as having DID were all most reluctant, fearful and ashamed of revealing their multiplicity. Indeed the anxiety inherent in disclosing the hidden system of multiplicity can be enormous, as the patient then feels profoundly vulnerable, their psychological survival threatened. The whole internal system can be thrown into turmoil by the very process of seeking psychotherapeutic help; fierce internal civil war can be unleashed as a battle arises between parts which are in favour of therapy and parts which are profoundly opposed to it. Any disclosure of the system to the therapist, or indeed to anyone, can be destabilizing because the system's inherent secrecy is thereby compromised; some parts will feel betrayed by the parts which disclose – and internal punishment may follow. This is not a picture of compliance leading to iatrogenesis. However, it could, to the naive observer, give the appearance of iatrogenesis because the alters may well become more apparent after disclosure to the therapist; once given the opportunity to talk and be listened to, there may be a clamouring to come forward. Even parts that are reluctant or hostile to the therapy may feel drawn, or 'bounced', into the quasi-political process – the negotiation between different parts with conflicting agendas and points of view.

On the other hand, I think there may be a kernel of truth in the iatrogenesis hypothesis. Some patients with DID are, in certain respects, very compliant. Indeed the strategy of developing alter personalities to adapt to whatever situation is presented is a kind of elaborate form of false self-compliance (Winnicott 1960). Moreover, since DID is not a biologically based disorder but a psychological creation, developed through processes of pretence, imagination and self-hypnosis, it would be surprising if its form and presentation were not variable and malleable. Patients with DID have had to learn to survive in dangerous and unpredictable interpersonal environments. They have, as a result, developed exceptionally sensitive and finely tuned antennae for the attitudes, desires and expectations of significant others, such as the therapist. Therefore some degree of moulding of presentation to suit the therapist may well occur. In acknowledging this, I must emphasize that in the absence of coercive or powerfully suggestive therapeutic regimes, I do not believe that DID is iatrogenic. What I do think is important is that the patient's behaviour and communications should be understood in the context of the therapeutic relationship – as is the case in all good therapy, especially that which is informed by psychoanalysis.

There is a further danger in a too easy embracing of the concept of DID. I have the impression that some who are not highly educated in psychiatry, or who lack extensive clinical experience, may apply the diagnosis to patients who might be better understood as suffering from anxiety or panic disorder or from schizophrenia. The fact that mental pathology, when it is not organically based, has an inherently plastic quality contributes to the ambiguity of diagnosis. Before arriving at a diagnosis of DID, the clinician should make a careful assessment of the patient's current mental state, history and development, and should look for the presence of a broad range of psychiatric symptoms.

Traumatic memory in DID: repression versus dissociation

Dissociative patients commonly show a combination of repression and dissociation of traumatic memory. As in the case of Liza, there will usually have been some continuous memory of traumatic abuse which then elaborates further. These further memories of trauma may emerge as sudden flashbacks, often precipitated by the woman having her own child, or by some new encounter with abuse or with the original abuser, or, paradoxically, when she feels safe for the first time (for example when in a supportive relationship).

The therapist may witness the patient switching into a child state of mind and recounting an experience of interpersonal trauma; on switching back into an adult state of mind, she may have little or no recollection of what had been reported. Who has remembered? Who had forgotten? This process is not in itself a description of repression or of its undoing. It is rather that what is known (whether memory or fantasy) in mental state A is not known in mental state B. B may become aware of A only through the mediation of the therapist. Whereas repression involves the division of the mind into a conscious and an unconscious area, dissociation involves a division of consciousness itself, resulting in a multiplicity of consciousnesses.

In those situations where the DID is initially latent, emerging only later in response to life events or talking in therapy, it is feasible also to describe the traumatized child states of mind as having been kept in a state of repression. Naturally, DID patients may in addition use any of the wide range of mental defences available to human beings.

A further distinction between repression and dissociation is that whereas the discernment of repression involves an *inference* – that a piece of conscious mental life gives disguised expression to a feeling, impulse or perception that is unacceptable to the conscious mind – dissociation is directly observable. Dissociation is observable either by the therapist who perceives the patient switching into different states of mind, or by the patient who reports dissociative experiences such as depersonalization. Dissociation itself can be such a prominent symptom that 'dissociative disorders' are listed in the DSM; repression, by contrast, is not directly observed or experienced and is not in itself a symptom: there are no 'repressive disorders' listed in the DSM.

Are the childhood memories of DID patients accurate? Memory is prone to error, is reconstructive rather than a veridical and fixed representation of reality, and is influenced by suggestion and a host of other psychodynamic factors (Mollon 1998). It seems possible that since DID is inherently a product of pretence, fantasy and self-hypnosis, the influence of confabulation could be particularly a factor in these conditions.

Liza's experience of alter personalities

One point which is apparent from Liza's account, and also from the editors' comments, is that her experience of her own multiplicity is not fixed but is continually changing. This is, I believe, absolutely typical. Since alter personalities are not biologically based or 'hard-wired' manifestations but are imaginative creations devised as strategies to cope with trauma, there is no reason why they should have any fixed quality. Liza appears to have evolved different personality states for different periods and tasks of life. The personalities have different experiences and different ages, and even different genders.

Liza also describes how the different selves have varying degrees of awareness of each other. This again seems quite typical. Interestingly, studies have shown that personality states which appear to have very limited *explicit* awareness of each other may nevertheless possess *implicit* (non-conscious) memory in common (for example Silberman *et al.* 1985; Freyd 1996).

The different selves may have conflicting views and agendas. This is illustrated in Liza's account of how one part is skilled at attracting men and likes to go out clubbing, but another part will want to get rid of the man. One part may put up with an unsatisfactory situation such as a marriage, for years, and then another part switches in and behaves quite differently.

Of course, every person feels and behaves differently at different times and in different situations. What distinguishes the experience and behaviour of the patient with DID is the *degree* of change and the sharpness of the transitions between behavioural states, as well as the personal experience of plurality.

Therapeutic considerations

It cannot be emphasized too strongly how frightened a person with DID can feel at the prospect of entering psychotherapy. The very fact of revealing the existence of the secret internal system to another human being can feel an enormous risk, like giving away protective secrets to a potential enemy. Beginning therapy may evoke an intense crisis and internal civil war. Some parts may be adamantly opposed to therapy, seeing no possibility of any good flowing from it; these parts may accuse those who have intiated the therapy of having betrayed the group.

The internal system of DID is a group, or a family, and must be approached as such. No matter what attitude is being expressed at any one moment, it is important to bear in mind that a number of other parts may be looking on, with quite different views. Inevitably the therapist is the focus of *multiple transferences*. Because the system is a group in conflict, the therapeutic work is political – a matter of facilitating negotiation and movement towards democracy. Any attempt by the therapist to impose a solution, or to work with only one part, is doomed to failure because other parts will sabotage any 'solution' to which they are not party.

The internal system of DID may show group processes and dynamics such as struggles for dominance and pecking order among the parts, alliances and sub-groupings, as well as projective identification. Processes of projection can be particularly dangerous when, for example, there is a locating in one part of all the feelings of despair, or of self-directed anger; this container can then become a kind of one-dimensional and unreflective suicide machine, which can be potentially lethal if it takes executive control.

While the DID system does function as a group, I think there must be care in how the therapist speaks to the patient about this. To speak of 'multiple personality' and of 'disorder' can sometimes seem to mirror and amplify the patient's sense of inner fragmentation. It is important to talk in such a way as also to acknowledge the inherent unity and coherence behind the apparent multiplicity.

To what extent integration or fusion is seen as a goal of therapy will vary according to the patient. Many will not view fusion or elimination of parts as at all desirable. Such a prospect may provoke intense anxiety and discord among the parts just as would be induced among the staff of an organization if it were announced that redundancies and 'downsizing' were imminent. For some patients a more feasible and acceptable goal is to work towards a state of being what John Southgate (1996) terms an 'associating multiple' in contrast with the state of 'dissociative multiple' – i.e. to attain greater association, communication and cooperation between parts. In this work a combination of the qualities of a family, group, organizational and individual therapist is required, as well as those of a political negotiator. The therapist must be absolutely honest and have integrity; he or she will be scrutinized with exquisite sensitivity by the patient who feels she is risking all by embarking on the therapy.

A common feature of the therapeutic process is what I call the crisis of trust. This begins with the patient's realization that the secrets are out, there is no going back and no shutting of Pandora's Box once it has been opened. The resulting panic experienced by the patient may be mirrored by a parallel anxiety on the part of the therapist; typical counter-transference reactions at this point are of feeling that it was a terrible error to have embarked on the therapeutic voyage. The patient's anxiety further accelerates at a point when child parts begin to press to come forward and tell their story. Paradoxically, the more trustworthy and understanding the therapist is felt to be, the more anxiety is evoked. This is because to trust is felt to be very dangerous. As the therapist appears willing to listen and empathize, more parts begin to wish to come forward. Vulnerable child parts may try to reach out to the therapist in trusting and naive ways, only to be thrust back by 'bouncers' whose 'job' is to protect the 'children'.

Above all, it is important to move at the patient's own pace and to be respectful of any need to close down or even withdraw from therapy. Coercive forms of therapy should definitely be avoided. These are people who are likely to have experienced much coercive abuse in childhood. Appropriate therapy must be profoundly respectful of the patient's autonomy. Coercive therapy may evoke compliance, but any apparent improvement would be superficial, and the danger of a worsening mental state is very real. Deliberate search for memories of trauma is likely to be experienced as violating and abusive, as well as carrying the danger of generating confabulated memories. Where there has been abuse in childhood, the phenomena of transference mean that the therapist will at times very readily be perceived as abusive or malevolent.

The attention to pacing is part of a wider concern with developing and protecting the patient's sense of safety. The loss of equilibrium which naturally occurs in therapy, as a result of talking and revealing the secret dissociative inner world, can be very frightening for the patient. Leaving the session in a traumatized and disoriented child state of mind is objectively dangerous, as well as terrifying for the patient. There needs to be discussion of what is tolerable and safe for the patient to experience in therapy and of what the therapist can do to reduce danger. For example, the patient may indicate that in the event of a crisis near to the end of a session, a particular personality part, characterized by adult competence, should be asked to take over.

In thinking about what I actually do in sessions with patients with DID, the activities seem to me quite complex. While addressing individual parts, it seems also important to take account of the patient as a whole and to assume that all parts are potentially listening. Thus it is still possible to explore transference, just as in ordinary individual therapy. The work can seem very similar to that of a group psychotherapist, who might talk to individual members, as well as to the group as a whole, and who might address the dynamics within the group as well as the relationship with the therapist, and might also attend to the setting, boundaries and ground rules of the group. To perceive the patient either as a multiplicity of parts or as a unity of personality are both incorrect. The patient is, paradoxically, both of these at the same time – and this paradox has to be tolerated and embraced.

I find that much of the time I am simply listening or facilitating communication between parts, rather than contributing an understanding of my own. In much of the patient's life, a particular part will undertake a particular function in a particular situation; what makes therapy very different is that all the parts potentially have their say to the therapist. Just by listening receptively and acceptingly, the therapist thereby acts as a focus of communication and integration. Often, but not always, interpretation of the kind that characterizes analytic work with non-dissociative patients seems irrelevant, since so much of the communicative and integrative work takes place through the reduction of dissociation inherent in talking to the therapist. One further activity that I do find necessary is clarifying and challenging the distorted thoughts and beliefs of particular parts. For example, abused child parts may display, in stark form, typical self-blame associated with victims of abuse. Other common distorted cognitions include the belief that one part can kill another part, by destroying the body, and can itself remain alive; and the belief that if an unwanted feeling is disowned and projected into another part, then the feeling is successfully disposed of.

A person who has been abused repeatedly within their childhood family will have suffered innumerable discouraging experiences, profoundly destructive of hope and self-esteem. As a general principle, I am inclined to the view that the more a person has suffered real trauma and deprivation in childhood, the more the therapy must include elements of support and encouragement. The patient will be exquisitely sensitive to whether the therapist really cares about her or is just applying a technique.

Summary and conclusions

The study of MPD/DID has never been part of the mainstream mental health disciplines of psychology, psychiatry or psychoanalysis. More recently, however, as the understanding of trauma and child abuse has developed, a new appreciation of the significance of dissociation is developing. DID seems to be a product of the combination of dissociation and imagination in the service of surviving repeated interpersonal trauma, from which there was no other means of escape. Although there may be some potential for DID to be influenced iatrogenically, this hypothesis does not account for the existence of those patients who present dissociatively without previous exposure to the idea of DID; usually, patients are extremely reluctant to reveal their secret dissociative internal world. As with all memories of childhood, the memory presentations of DID patients may contain a mixture of truth and confabulation. Therapeutic methods aimed specifically at memory recovery are not recommended because of the two dangers of fostering pseudo-memories and retraumatizing the patient. Entering psychotherapy may be extremely frightening for the DID patient and may be destabilizing. The dissociative system behaves in some ways like a group; a style of work which combines individual, group, family and organizational psychotherapy is required. By being receptive to the communications from various parts of the dissociative patient, the psychotherapist and the therapy setting become a focus of integration. Fusion of parts is often not seen as a desirable or feasible goal by DID patients. Instead, the goal might be to facilitate the achievement of a state of being an associating (as opposed to dissociating) multiple person. Therapy with DID should be characterized by caution, support and encouragement.

References

Aldridge-Morris, R. (1989) *Multiple Personality Disorder. An Excercise in Deception.* Hove: Erlbaum.

Cohen, D. (1996) *Alter Egos. Multiple Personalities.* London: Constable.

Fairbairn, R. (1952) *Psychoanalytic Studies of the Personality.* London: Routledge.

Freyd, J. J. (1996) *Betrayal Trauma. The Logic of Forgetting Childhood Abuse.* Cambridge, MA: Harvard University Press.

Hacking, I. (1995) *Rewriting the Soul. Multiple Personality and the Sciences of Memory.* Princeton, NJ: Princeton University Press.

Herman, J. and van der Kolk, B. (1987) Traumatic antecedents of borderline personality disorder, in B. A. van der Kolk (ed.) *Psychological Trauma.* Washington, DC: American Psychiatric Press.

Horowitz, M. (1978) *Stress Response Syndromes.* New York: Jason Aronson.

Kernberg, O. (1975) *Borderline Conditions and Pathological Narcissism.* New York: Jason Aronson.

Kluft, R. P. (1994) Multiple personality disorder: observations on the etiology, natural history, recognition, and resolution of a long-neglected condition, in R. M. Klein and B. K. Doone (eds) *Psychological Concepts and Dissociative Disorders.* Hillsdale, NJ: Erlbaum.

Masters, B. (1997) *She Must Have Known.* London: Corgi.

Mollon, P. (1996) *Multiple Selves, Multiple Voices. Working With Trauma, Violation and Dissociation.* Chichester: Wiley.

Mollon, P. (1998) *Remembering Trauma. A Psychotherapist's Guide to Memory and Illusion.* Chichester: Wiley.

Putman, F. W. (1989) *Diagnosis and Treatment of Multiple Personality Disorder.* New York: Guildford.

Rosenfeld, H. (1971) A clinical approach to the psychoanalytic theory of life and death instincts: an investigation into the aggressive aspects of narcissism, *International Journal of Psycho-Analysis*, 52: 169–78.

Ross, C. (1989) *Multiple Personality Disorder. Diagnosis, Clinical Features and Treatment.* New York: Wiley.

Salter, A. C. (1995) *Transforming Trauma.* Thousand Oaks, CA: Sage.

Silberman, E. K., Putnam, F. W., Weingartner, H., Braun, B. G. and Post, R. M. (1985) Dissociative states in multiple personality disorder: a quantitative study, *Psychiatry Research*, 15: 253–60.

Southgate, J. (1996) An attachment perspective on dissociation and multiplicity. Paper presented for the third annual John Bowlby Memorial Lecture, 23–24 February 1996 (available from The Centre for Attachment-based Psychoanalytic Psychotherapy.)

Spanos, N. P. (1996) *Multiple Identities and False Memories. A Sociocognitve Perspective.* Washington, DC: American Psychological Association.

Ulman, R. B. and Brothers, D. (1988) *The Shattered Self. A Psychoanalytic Study of Trauma.* Hillsdale, NJ: Analytic Press, Erlbaum.

van der Kolk, B., van der Hart, O. and Marmar, C. (1996) Dissociation and information processing in posttraumatic stress disorder, in B. van der Kolk, A. McFarlane and L. Weisaeth (eds) *Traumatic Stress.* New York: Guildford.

Winnicott, D. (1960) Ego distortion in terms of true and false self, in *The Maturational Processes and the Facilitating Environment.* New York: International Universities Press.

Wyre, R. (1987) *Working with Sex Offenders.* Oxford: Perry Publications.

Chapter 5

Multiple personalities: a cautionary note

Graz Kowszun

Introduction

My interest in childhood abuse and multiple personality is rooted personally. I was a client before I became a counsellor and psychotherapist. Brought up in an immigrant family devastated by the Second World War, I felt an outsider from an early age, confused by cultural norms, and inadequately parented in a traumatized and marginalized refugee family. Subsequently, the experience of growing up lesbian in two heterosexist cultures and three years of sexual abuse by a male neighbour ensured that my childhood left me feeling distressed, fearful, shame-bound and unintegrated in my sense of self.

Recognizing I needed help, I entered Reichian bodywork therapy while still at college and this was followed by a decade of diverse therapies, each more or less helpful and frustrating, all of which taught me overlapping languages and approaches to my inner world. Nobody suggested I suffered from multiple personalities – it was not fashionable – although I did work on polarities in gestalt, splitting in analytic psychotherapy, Parent, Adult and Child in Transactional Analysis (TA), and sub-personalities in psychosynthesis (Rowan and Cooper 1998).

As a result of my experiences, I know deep within that psychotherapy and counselling can be vital healing experiences, but they do not always yield a positive result. I have learnt about changing fashions in therapy and how good intentions do not always make up for partial understanding. Human beings are complex creatures, and as healers our understanding and wisdom are limited. I do not regret getting involved in therapy, but some of the lessons I have learnt have not been those the practitioner intended.

Professionally, I moved from social work to counselling and integrative psychotherapy, specializing in work with adult survivors of childhood abuse, people with substance abuse problems, issues of identity, the culturally different and lesbian, gay and bisexual clients. Over the last 15 years, I have worked in some depth with about 50 survivors of childhood abuse and neglect and about 1000 clients altogether. Some survivors clearly remember and own their experience from the start, while others are unsure what is memory and what are odd images or feeling states, and may vacillate in their self-descriptions. I have had clients who have insisted there was no abuse in the face of what seems to me to be overwhelming subjective evidence, and other clients who present as survivors and then change their minds.

Up to now, I have not found a particular need to introduce a concept of multiple personality to my clients. This could be because of my doubts about the value of so doing and because my integrative framework appears not to need this addition. I do not expect uniformity and singularity in others and so my dialogue with clients may include reference to persona, roles, ego states and parts of self without tying us to a particular view of how the self is structured. Where clients introduce the idea and suggest they may be multiple personalities, I accept and explore this as part of how they see themselves at the time, without giving it special significance. I may even counterbalance their sense of disunity and multiplicity by focusing on the many ways in which they have a unified sense of self. To date, this appears adequate as a response, although I remain open to clients expressing different needs in the future.

The sceptical arguments

There are many grounds on which the concept of multiple personality and its therapeutic application have been contested. Firstly, there are six viewpoints from which I want to distance myself:

1 Strong trauma is unforgettable

There are those who deny that people can repress memories of strong traumatic experiences, such as childhood abuse (for example Loftus and Ketchum 1994), claiming those memories stand out as most vivid and unforgettable. According to this view, memories cannot be recovered as they cannot be 'forgotten' in the first place. If repression of such memories is deemed impossible, there is no need to conceptualize different forms of repression such as the division of memories among many multiple personalities. This argument is part of the 'recovered memory debate' and has been thoroughly repudiated elsewhere (Walker 1996; McGuire 1997).

2 People are single, unified and unvarying

Western individualist philosophy 'posits a single unified, unvarying subject of experiences in every human breast' (Radden 1996: 5–6). I disagree. Experiences ranging from loss of consciousness during sleep, through incongruence between what is spoken and what is communicated non-verbally, in absent-mindedness or through ambivalence, to 'acting completely out of character' are everyday experiences of normal living (Rowan and Cooper 1998). At times, I have found working with polarities (see Perls 1992; Polster 1995) or sub-personalities (see Assagioli 1965; Rowan 1990) extremely useful with a broad range of clients, at various levels of functioning.

3 Clients cannot be believed

Some practitioners (for example Aldridge-Morris 1989) dismiss multiplicity on the basis that clients are psychotic or stupid malingerers, or for whatever reason are simply not to be believed. While I am aware that personal truths tend to change in the course of time, I keep an open mind and hold no truck with defining people and dismissing them out of hand.

4 Rejection of regression

Dismissing regression as a false phenomenon and an example of irresponsibility or dramatic play-acting on the part of the client is another rejection of multiplicity. I believe a certain amount of regression is common to most people under stress, particularly when we are over-identified with our feelings, and perhaps overwhelmed (Sandler and Freud 1985).

5 Rejection of dissociation

There are those who reject the concept of dissociation as unnecessary and unhelpful. I find it a useful descriptor of an impact of trauma, though the term can create confusion (see van der Kolk and Fisler 1995) by being used in different ways. I describe dissociation as a state of mind akin to panic, where I am isolated from my capacity to connect with others or even to find words to describe my inner experiences at the time. Flashbacks, a silent emptiness accompanied at times by feelings of fear, powerlessness and shame may all be present.

6 Biochemical explanations of mental illness and denial of the reality and impact of sexual abuse

There are many psychiatrists who are not convinced by multiplicity nor particularly interested in a patient's life experiences, and who view patients presenting in this way as suffering from a biochemical imbalance. They tend to apply a diagnosis of schizophrenia, depression or bipolar mood disorder and medicate the individual accordingly. This may be with the best of intentions, the result of being busy, of a belief in biological reductionism, lack of training in psychotherapeutic method, lack of knowledge of child abuse and its effects or for other reasons. Unfortunately, some mental health practitioners, including psychiatrists, psychoanalysts and behavioural therapists, have had a history of lamentably bad practice when working with survivors of childhood abuse, and perhaps the situation has not improved appreciably in recent years (Walker 1992; Armstrong 1996).

There are, however, other problems with the diagnosis and treatment of multiple personalities which, in my view, are more substantive.

1 The social construction of psychology

Given that psychological knowledge and understanding are ways of making sense of – and thus going beyond – experience, they can be understood as emerging from a socio-historical process of competition among professionals, whereby 'psychology constitutes its object in the process of knowing it' (Rose 1996: 49) This process of contestation has been described as a power battle among interest groups on issues such as which articles to publish, which themes to accept for conferences, and which viewpoint holds sway in the latest diagnostic manual or in national organizations representing the therapeutic profession (see Kuhn 1962; Foucault 1972). For instance, Cornelia B. Wilbur's attempts to publish scholarly articles about multiple personalities were blocked for decades until 1984, 11 years after her client Sybil became the prototypical multiple personality (Schreiber 1973), whereas more recently whole books on multiplicity have been published.

As a sociologist studying psychotherapeutic power, Rose (1996) writes about the social construction of theories of our inner worlds, showing how they are not universal but developed to suit particular social orders. He draws our attention to how people in the West currently and typically see themselves in ways that precisely suit the global market economy we have created. Thus we 'invent' ourselves as free individuals with an inner world, capable of autonomy, choice and responsibility; interested in self-awareness, self-control and self-actualization. In other societies, perhaps, more collectivist, spiritual and duty-bound views of personality dominate (Lago and Thompson 1996). When problems arise, we call upon the 'psy' experts (psychoanalysts, psychologists, psychotherapists, psychiatrists, etc.) for their help, and rely upon their vocabularies and techniques, which shape our senses of identity whether we are in therapy or not.

Examining multiple personality in this light, it could be argued that the concept simplifies the experience of those who grow up in extremely abusive contexts and then find the demands of contemporary liberal democracies alien and difficult. By imposing a norm of personhood as a distinct organized and integrated centre of awareness, feeling, evaluation and agency in the world, we are discounting most prevalent cultural ways of being, as well as disregarding how gendered are our notions of individuality. We are assuming the universal template for personhood is a stereotypical white Protestant middle class heterosexual and able-bodied male, and failing to see how the family, the ancestors or Mother Earth can function as the centre of understanding, motivation and evaluation for many. Through this process we make problems out of those who do not fit our singular norm. Furthermore, by describing a distinct disorder, as 'psy' practitioners, we are claiming the authority and technical skill to diagnose and intervene.

2 How problem definitions are negotiated interpersonally

Having suggested how on the macro level the whole edifice of human psychology is socially constructed, we can then examine this process more specifically. Michael Balint (1964), thinking about general practitioners, described how a GP and patient will reach agreement on diagnoses defining what is wrong and how it should be treated. Others such as Frank (1973) compare different systems of persuasion and healing and examine the commonalities, such as the therapist and client forming a supportive relationship, agreeing a frame of reference to give meaning to the particular distress or problem and participating together in healing rituals, contributing a sense of mastery and success. According to this view, multiple personality may be partly or wholly iatrogenic, that is, diagnosed 'because of an interaction between the needs of the patient and the goals of the therapist' (Levitt 1988).

3 Is multiplicity best understood psychologically or sociologically?

The history of MPD in the West in the twentieth century has been influenced by psychoanalysis and behaviourism as these replaced religious treatment of 'possession'. Janet's interest in dissociation and multiple personality (1907), and his theory linking hypnotic susceptibility with weak identity or dissociation, seemed almost to disappear until the 1970s. Hacking (1995: 39) picks up the story from there: 'In the coarse measure of decades, the multiple movement germinated in the sixties, emerged in the seventies, matured in the eighties, and is adapting itself to new environments in the nineties.' It was Cornelia B. Wilbur's analysis of *Sybil*, described by Schreiber (1973) that captured the imagination of lay person and professional alike. Since then, Kluft (cited in Hacking 1995) has described how theories of the aetiology of MPD draw upon virtually every psychological theory known, from primitive wish fulfilment to unhomogenized introjections.

Professional literature in the late 1970s increasingly featured MPD, and charismatic therapists such as Wilbur and Allison spread their 'oral literature' on multiplicity. In 1980 the establishment of a learned society (the International Society for the Study of Multiple Personality and Dissociation) coincided with the American Psychiatric Association's inclusion of dissociative disorders and MPD in the third edition of their *Diagnostic and Statistical Manual of Mental Disorders* (DSM III 1980). Other factors that Kluft (1994) cites as contributing to the mushrooming in diagnosis of MPD include the study of post-traumatic stress disorder following the Vietnam War, and the influence of feminism, which exposed the prevalence of sexual abuse. Such burgeoning pressures within society and the psychotherapeutic professions appear not to be enough for some evangelical therapists and self-help activists, who seem to need to add personal pressure on clients, as suggested by the following: '60% of multiples will not do or say anything that suggests MPD unless subjected to a detailed, subtle, and sophisticated dissociative inquiry. Never accept "No" for an answer. Denial, forgetting and minimisation produce many false "no's" to questions regarding dissociative experiences' (Barker 1992).

I find it rather chilling to read that in the United States multiplicity is now considered as common as anxiety and mood disorders, and almost as widespread as substance abuse (Hocking and Company 1992: vii): 'Today, studies indicate that MPD in fact affects about 1% of adults in the general population, and ... about 10% ... [have] had a dissociative disorder at some time in their lives.' I wonder if it will spread similarly in the UK?

My reservations are summed up by Spanos:

The historical changes in the prevalence of MPD, the substantial national differences in prevalence and in gender ratios, and the large differences in the frequency with which different clinicians make the diagnosis are difficult to account for parsimoniously in terms of a disease perspective. They are, however, reminiscent of the historical changes in the prevalence of demonic possession, the large cross-cultural differences in the prevalence of spirit possession, and the large differences in rates of glossolalia [speaking in tongues] seen between different churches in North America. In short, the prevalence data for MPD suggest that MPD, like possession phenomena, is a social creation that varies in frequency as a function of the expectations for its occurrence that are transmitted to patients. The most important sources of such expectations are therapists committed to the MPD diagnosis, but other sources (for example media) have become increasingly important as information about MPD has infused into the wider culture.

(Spanos 1994: 152)

4 How particular clients and therapists may then be susceptible to negotiating a multiple personality diagnosis

If we view diagnosis as socially constructed, what may predispose some clients and professionals to diagnose multiple personality? One factor which cannot be dismissed is habit, for it would appear that some therapists never encounter a case of MPD while others diagnose them frequently. Hacking (1995: 270) suggests people 'may observe with some justice that the most reliable predictor of the occurrence of multiple personality is a clinician who diagnoses and treats multiples'.

Identification may be another factor. Perry (cited in Spanos 1994) suggests that more than one in six therapists in the USA who work with MPD have previously been diagnosed with a dissociative disorder themselves. Neither should we ignore our narcissistic susceptibility to the desire to gain attention and be 'special'. MPD is exciting, exotic and unusual. It captures our imagination. As therapists, we may listen selectively or use our powers of influence to reinforce, however subtly, particular themes or self-perceptions in our clients. I have heard about the very special treatment a homeless woman received from a voluntary agency when she declared herself both multiple and a survivor of ritual abuse. Apparently no efforts were spared to find her 24-hour befriending, high quality, high support accommodation, and special funds for a laptop computer. She was even allocated two counsellors at the same time as it was considered too traumatic and dangerous for one to bear her story alone!

The possibility that some clients and therapists may be prone to dramatic expressions, to 'acting out', even to deceit, is a difficult one to raise. Yet these are normal ways of behaving. Pretence, make-believe and the overlap between fantasy and reality feature to some degree in most adult–child relationships. The prevalence of affairs in apparently monogamous couples, the acceptance of the 'white lie' and, on a different level, the secrets and deceit involved in most forms of abuse, both of children and adults, suggest it may be naive to discount the role of exaggeration and lying in our professional lives.

There is also the issue of coping patterns or defence styles. It is common for some abused children or young people to experience a heady mixture of excitement and fear as they became an exotic object for someone with the authority to define and exploit. Being exotic can become a self image which protects the young person from awareness of her or his inner pain, and thus a defence or coping pattern that can persist into adulthood and therapy. Could a diagnosis such as multiplicity, which is both exciting and frightening, be appealing? And encourage some individuals to adapt their self concept and behaviour to fit it better? If the therapist reveals some interest in multiple personalities, whether verbally or non-verbally, this may function as suggestion. This view is supported by research that shows multiplicity to be suggestible in psychological experiments (Spanos 1994).

5 Analogies and absolutes

It is also worth bearing in mind the danger of the reification of concepts which are meant figuratively, but come to be understood literally. In our culture, we are prone to perceiving objects and structures as absolute rather than as more fluid processes. We limit and constrain our sense of our responsibility for how we relate to and understand the concept. While some of us may be drawn to a holistic perspective on human health, for others the complex interplay between psyche and soma blurs the line between what is figurative and what is literal. For instance, from a body or process psychology perspective a client's desire to get something off her chest but difficulty in doing so may be reflected in her use of shallow breathing to suppress tears of grief. It is worth considering the degree to which we see certain aspects of a client's story as significant. The psychological use of the concept of trauma, the positing of the existence of the unconscious, and the search for a biological base for addiction are all examples of how ideas, questions and the search for meaning turn into absolutes that define, rather than explorations which guide.

6 The vagueness and changeability of definitions of multiplicity and how they relate to theories of personality and memory

Hacking (1995) describes how current concepts differ from those prevalent before the 1970s. Then multiple personalities tended to be limited to two personalities rather than tens or hundreds; equal numbers of men and women were diagnosed; alters did not claim to be of a different race or gender to the host; and they were not characters out of TV soap operas. Neither were they animals or otherwise non-human, and links were not generally made to a history of abuse, etc. Since the 1970s the picture has changed to a much more dramatic type of presentation, and debates about nomenclature also reflect greater interest in the subject. These debates about naming, from multiple personality disorder (MPD), back to Dissociative Identity Disorder (DID) in DSM IV, reflect an argument about whether to stress distinct personalities or to view the condition as one of fragmentation. David Spiegel (1993) writes: 'There is a widespread misunderstanding of the essential psychopathology in this dissociative disorder, which is a failure of integration of various aspects of identity, memory and consciousness. The problem is not having more than one personality; it is having less than one personality.' The opposing view in its radical form is that not only are there people with multiple personalities, but integration is neither necessary nor desirable (Hocking and

Company 1992). Instead, proponents of this view argue for a political movement for recognizing 'households' of personalities as a legitimate way of life, with therapy aimed at encouraging cooperative functioning among alters.

The self-help movement, which has a very strong presence on the Internet, has created a sub-culture that exasperates many professionals, as Kluft demonstrates:

> Part of the socially prescribed role of being ill is working to recover and leave your illness behind. We are in a position where many of our MPD patients and some of us ourselves are not necessarily bearing this in mind. Instead we are giving license to a lot of MPD patients sitting round learning how to deal with an MPD environment, making MPD friends, talking MPD all day . . .
>
> (Hacking 1995: 38)

Returning to the official definition of what is currently described as dissociative identity disorder (DSM IV, APA 1994: 477–91), it is interesting to note that the essential features are defined rather sparsely, there being only four: the presence of relatively enduring identities which recurrently take control of the person's behaviour, with amnesia that is not due to substance abuse, disease or children's fantasy.

Arguably, the first two points could be applied to everyone or no one, depending on how they are understood. Views of identity, personality and agency vary enormously among psychotherapists. For instance Clarkson (1992: 175–203), writing about one approach to psychotherapy – Transactional Analysis – identifies six interrelated concepts of the self, some singular, others varying, all healthy and normal. Daniel Stern, the eminent developmentalist, describes four senses of self, which persist over the life span (Stern 1985); while Harry Stack Sullivan (1953) describes personality as a relatively stable pattern of relatedness determined by the stability of our interpersonal environment, thereby defining it interpersonally and flexibly. The question remains: what is meant by 'presence' and taking 'control' in the DSM IV definition? For this to have any real significance it needs a much tighter and clearer explanation. It is simply too general to be of any use.

In exploring the inability to recall, we can be heading into the realms of the recovered memory debate (see, for instance, Walker 1996; McGuire 1997), or we may simply refer to the common psychological defence of repression. Neither of these are unique to multiple personality. This does, however, raise general questions about how we conceptualize memory. For instance, it is relatively well known that memory is mood-specific; that stress impairs memory function; and that the reliability of a memory is influenced by the personal feelings and meanings attached to it, the age of the person at the time of the event and the circumstances and prompts offered for remembering (see, for instance, McGuire 1997). The American Psychiatric Association is careful to exclude malingering for gain and factitious disorder where there may be a pattern of help-seeking behaviour; but how are diagnosers to discriminate between claimed and authentic lack of memory? Or to distinguish inability to remember from unwillingness to do so? Finally, some psychologists, philosophers and social scientists are questioning the aetiological relationship between our past and our present behaviour. They suggest that understanding multiplicity in terms of childhood abuse is a retrospective assumption that encourages unhappy people towards a particular self-definition. Thus Hacking writes (1995: 88): 'A certain picture of origins is imparted to disturbed and unhappy people, who then use it to reorder or reorganize their conception of their past. It becomes their past.'

I find it odd that the essential diagnostic features are so limited and inconclusive. All the descriptors in the general text of DSM IV are reduced, as it were, to 'flavour text'. At the very least this suggests there is a great variety in experiences of multiple personality, or very little consensus among the definers of mental disorder. Given that almost anyone can be made to fit the category, such a definition then leaves individual practitioners free to apply the diagnosis if and when they wish: they will not be bound to satisfy strict criteria.

Among the attributes suggested in the general description of Dissociative Identity Disorder are several that these practitioners may draw upon:

1 The presence of a host personality carrying the individual's given name, which is usually 'passive, dependent, guilty and depressed'.
2 This is accompanied by alternate identities of different ages and genders, with different names, memories, temperaments, who may have emerged in specific circumstances and be more or less prominent.
3 The number of identities tends to be under ten, but some individuals claim more than a hundred.
4 These personalities are often in conflict with each other, and may vie for access to consciousness, even by producing hallucinations.
5 There is often a reported history of severe physical and sexual abuse in childhood. Some clients also have adult histories of abuse and battery.
6 Other accompanying symptoms may include suicide attempts, self-harm, impulsiveness, sudden dramatic mood changes, aggression, and also post-traumatic reactions such as nightmares, startle responses and flashbacks.
7 Claims have been made on many occasions for some unusual abilities such as pain control, variations in physiological function across personalities, and high degrees of hypnotizability.

These features paint a much more graphic picture of multiplicity. However, apart from the last most contentious point, they could equally apply at times to a large proportion of the survivors of abuse whom I have known. For instance, (4) can be thought of as referring to states of regression and the critical attitude of the superego to them, while (2) and (3) could apply to the second of Clarkson's concepts of self, which she calls ego states or functional roles. And even with (7) I have on many occasions been astounded by the bizarre, even the apparently impossible, and have reminded myself that our knowledge of the connections between psyche and soma is very limited. Thus, as I grapple with the bases of what distinguishes multiple personality from other more commonplace conditions, it becomes even more elusive, with the categorical features appearing to run through my fingers like sand.

7 Questionable claims of scientific status

Hacking (1994) effectively questions the various attempts made by therapists to establish the scientific basis of multiplicity, appearing to turn it into an object of knowledge. For instance, he shows how research findings used to support the various diagnostic questionnaires have been distorted, depending on the views of those already running treatment centres. The questionnaires themselves are extremely direct and so easily faked (Gilbertson *et al.* 1992). No independent calibration was carried out; instead prior expert diagnoses were used to 'validate' them.

8 Ethical and existential concerns about responsibility

Given the difficulty of pinning down MPD and the complexities of understanding the meaning of 'sameness' and 'change' when considering personality, it may be relevant to consider the possible advantages and costs of adopting the concept in terms of personal and social responsibility. For instance, multiplicity confers certain advantages in enabling the disavowal of difficult emotions and the maintenance of close relationships with perpetrators and family members or other adults who failed in their duty to protect. Thus, the loving daughter remains separate from the horrified, enraged and grief-struck daughter who was abused, and the individual can maintain the illusion of a close family. Like intoxication, or indeed the use of hypnosis, multiplicity can distance us from reprehensible behaviour, with claims that '"I" wasn't myself when I committed that crime or acted contrary to my self-perception.'

There is one further aspect where I agree with Hacking (1995: 266–7), which perhaps reflects more of a moral standpoint. I fear multiple personality therapy does more to alienate clients from their humanness than it does to heal them, leading to a false consciousness rather than a deep self-knowledge. Avoiding self-ascription of acts that one agrees were not carried out by anybody else is a form of self-deception, on various levels (Radden 1996). If a part of me does not know what another part of me knows, am I literally deceiving myself? If I go to therapy wanting to lead a more successful life and spend the next *x* years dividing and then possibly integrating, my self concept, will my life have improved or am I also deceiving myself that I am getting better? I suspect – though I cannot show – that these are acts of self-deception: blocks to intimacy or intrapersonal and interpersonal contact as Erskine (1997) would say. Ultimately it is this gut reaction that disturbs me most.

9 A feminist critique of multiplicity

More recently feminists such as Rivera (1991) and Leys (1992) have argued that multiplicity keeps women in a victim role: sick, damaged, passive, and dissociating from their wishes to act outside of socially prescribed feminine roles. For instance, in the prototypical internal 'household' the strong protector role is often taken by the stereotypically male personality role, while the lesbian is minimalized in relation to the heterosexual host personality, who thus denies sexual feelings towards women.

10 A predilection for client and counsellor to stress what is discordant over what is integrated

As a psychotherapist, I see value in differentiation before integration, for instance in a couple, or in someone coming to terms with their race and culture, gender or sexual orientation. However, to define closely a range of multiple identities, giving each one an age, personality traits, different emotions, skills and preferences, is to underline differences rigidly, rather than stressing all the other aspects of identity that are integrated as a basis for a core sense of self. My reading suggests that while there are some clients who find a diagnosis of MPD illuminating and a relief, many find it a deeply shocking, even traumatizing experience (see, for instance, Cohen *et al.* 1991). Recent guidelines for treating DID published by the International Society for the Study of Dissociation (1994) state: 'It is counterproductive to urge the patient to create additional alternate personalities, to urge alternate personalities to adopt names when they have none, or to urge that alternate personalities function in a more elaborated and autonomous way than they already are functioning in the patient.' However, these guidelines are not necessarily well known or heeded, and furthermore, the self-help movement often functions independently, as attested by the numerous sites on the World Wide Web.

11 A predilection for multiplicity to be linked with the bizarre and far-fetched

Although it does not affect the issue of the existence or utility of multiplicity directly, the way in which multiplicity continues to be linked with questionable notions, experiences and behaviours raises questions about the soundness of other claims that some multiples may make. Examples are those related to possession and exorcism rituals; to hypnotism and sodium amytal interviews; and more recently to the very high rates of association with Satanic worship that have been claimed in America. The latter suggests that up to a quarter of multiples have been ritually abused, yet, as Putman writes (1993: 85), 'despite almost a decade of sensational allegations, no independent evidence has emerged to corroborate these claims'.

I wonder if Chris Sizemore, the multiple described in *The Three Faces of Eve* (Thigpen and Cleckley 1957) may have started a new trend when in 1989 she claimed she had past life alters, present with her since before birth. There are certainly bizarre and far-fetched claims of animal personalities and stereotypes which are sexist and racist, and clearly highly influenced by the media. Thus, according to Elaine Showater in an article in *The Observer Review* (14 June 1998), 'one woman confessed she had made up an alter called Nikki because everyone else in her MPD support group had one and she felt left out'.

By identifying a considerable range of sceptical arguments against multiplicity, I hope I have encouraged an attitude of caution by practitioners. My intention has not been to insult individuals like Liza, who consider themselves to be multiple, nor to discount the meaning and value such a self concept has for them. If none the less I have offended some people, I regret this.

Liza

My professional value base is humanistic and intersubjective. I believe in inviting clients to trust their experience and process in our relationship as the source of healing. I also trust my own in so far as I choose to share persistent reactions, inviting clients to make of them what they will. I accept a client's self-definition at a particular time as our baseline, and have no vested interest in establishing that any particular form of abuse, neglect, trauma or other wounding did or did not take place in their past.

As I read the transcript of Liza's public story, I perceive a range of data, as well as missing the qualities of voice tone, non-verbal communication, body language, and most important the relationship, which would alter significantly the communication that might take place. I am informed by the content of what Liza says, the themes she emphasizes and what she skates over or omits; by what I can glean of her style of speech and how it changes, the order in which she covers items, and my emotional, physical, intuitive and cognitive reactions to what is said; and also by my overall impressions. Liza strikes me as a woman who has great courage, but who is also very scared; a woman of imagination and insight, who is also confused and who jumps to conclusions. She is a woman of wisdom and maturity as well as youthful in her lack of appreciation of how uncertain, ambivalent, changeable and contradictory we all tend to be. I am aware of the context of our communication, and this makes me a little uncomfortable: neither she nor I are simply subjects, but we both have an impersonal function: Liza is apparently the illustrative example of a multiple personality and I the sceptic. We do not have a real relationship, nor a history: we are unlikely to meet in person.

Were we working together therapeutically, I might share my perceptions as well as hunches and understanding with Liza, both in pursuit of her goals and also as a way of developing clarity and depth in our relationship. I would be very careful in my use of myself, particularly in the earlier stages of relationship, and I would devote the majority of time to closely tracking Liza within her own frame of reference. Warner (1997) writes about fragile process, in a way which dovetails with Kohutian (1984) self-psychological insights into approaching people with an injured sense of themselves. This is achieved by offering a lot of empathy and validation, and by refraining from challenge or interpretation.

I trust that Liza might want to communicate with me and has some investment in healing or resolving blocks to living better. I will put my best efforts into grasping the communication(s) and supporting this investment, while recognizing that the ulterior goals of therapy are not always and necessarily healing (see Steiner 1990; Clarkson 1992). As it is, I am not aware of her goals nor of what she wants from therapy, and I consider this vital to find out, as it will guide our work. I am not aware of how comfortable or not Liza is with her disclosures. I am grateful she has revealed these aspects of her experience and inner world, for the purposes of this book, and I hope it has not cost her dearly.

The gestalt psychotherapist James Kepner (1995) describes a useful developmental sequence for working with survivors of abuse. First, he suggests, a client needs to deal with isolation, shame and trust issues through building self and environmental support structures; and we need to establish and maintain a therapeutic alliance. Next, clients may need help to learn to manage feelings, boundaries and finding a pace that does not overwhelm or lead to dissociation. Only then is it useful for clients to express and remember instances of abuse in Kepner's third phase: undoing retroflections and full mourning, before moving on to the final phase of reconsolidation: developing an interweaving transcendent context of meaning to life, that is sufficient to hold and give meaning to the experience of abuse.

I wonder about Liza in terms of Kepner's model. What stages of healing has she reached and what tasks lie ahead in the short or long run? I would want to check with Liza more closely whether she has post-traumatic stress symptomatology (persistent re-experiencing of childhood abuse scenes, avoidance of associations with this, and symptoms of increased arousal, DSM IV 1994); and how she manages stress, feelings and memories. Does she, for instance, get overwhelmed, over-reactive or confused between past and current experiences? Regressive experiences suggest this is a significant source of distress for her. I value the Transactional Analysis model of ego states (for example Woolams and Brown 1978; Clarkson 1992) and believe that we do move out of our Adult here-and-now persona into earlier states (Child ego states) and those (Parent ego states) we have introjected from others. With clients who struggle frequently with regressive experiences that put them in danger, I teach them to spot and contain these until they are in safer surroundings (Stuart 1997).

In more general ways, I will enquire early on how Liza sees herself and how she cares for herself. Does she ask for the support she needs, and is she generally on her own side? Her tendency seems to be to express herself in a passive way and to make statements such as 'just incapable of looking after myself and doing what I want to do'; and 'I've just gone from chaos to chaos to chaos'. This belies and discounts how she successfully tackled dependence on medication and alcohol and revolutionized her attitude and behaviour with her children. It suggests that Liza does not give herself credit where it is due, for instance for her great fortitude and achievements; and this may reinforce an underlying sense of shame (Kaufman 1989).

In terms of acknowledging her abuse, I wonder how she views herself as a survivor. Perhaps she denies it at times or intellectualizes it, for instance when visiting her parents. On other occasions it may be that her orientation is mainly to her past, attributing everything to her abuse. She appears to disavow feelings of anger, and that is a difficult emotion for many women and most survivors.

I will not be encouraging Liza to focus on her past until she is reliably able to support and manage herself in a non-traumatizing way. In Berne's terminology (1961), Liza may have strong stimulus hunger – a need for much intensity in her life. Underneath this, how isolated and shame-bound is she? On a day-to-day level, is she able to pace herself and modulate the intensity of her experiences so they are tolerable?

I will want to explore with Liza to what extent she had basic self-support tools, such as responding kindly to her own needs for food, rest, relaxation and exercise. I may check whether she is familiar with and uses relaxation methods, and whether she knows how to 'ground', through focusing on her body and her breathing, and what she is presently registering in awareness through her five senses. For instance, I will encourage her to learn those skills and methods where they are weak or absent, and I anticipate that regular chunks of our session time will be taken up with such self-management and interpersonal skills work in response to what she brings to sessions of her day-to-day life.

I recognize that Liza's relationship to her own body is problematic. Her attention and her pain is strongly focused on the physical plane: she describes feeling dirty, picking at her skin; she does not eat well, she has various aches and pains, is frequently ill, and suffers from palpitations and panic attacks. I will encourage her to take small but consistent steps to transform her relationship to her body, and may challenge her belief that full understanding must precede behavioural change.

From what I can gather, Liza appears to be somewhere between the support phase and the self-functions phase in Kepner's model of healing tasks. In our work together, I want us to focus initially on establishing a relationship, addressing issues of trust, boundaries, safety and containment, both in therapy and in her own self-management. I will be listening actively to what she wants to tell me and also enquiring about her social support; whether she keeps good boundaries and has non-abusive friends. I will, for example, ask more about her current relationship with her family of origin. I will also want to encourage her to manage safety and boundary issues that are interpersonal. Does she have assertiveness skills such as being able to say 'no' or 'yes' according to her feelings and needs?

I do not imagine work with Liza will proceed smoothly: healing from abuse is rarely a gentle process. I doubt if all parts of her will be willing and able to negotiate and then commit themselves to a suitable contract with me (Sills 1997) which will hold Liza safely, particularly as I have publicly expressed doubts about the usefulness of her self-attributed diagnosis.

Were we not known to each other, how would we fare in the messiness of two ordinary fallible women getting to know each other? What hopes and dreads might Liza develop as she lets her feelings and needs emerge in our relationship and experiences my responses? With all the lies and betrayal she has experienced, as well as the loss of dear ones through death, it could take years for us to develop the mutual trust and love for Liza to experience deeply and to use the support and contact I can offer by attuning to her in different relationship modalities (Clarkson 1996):

- to understand her social context and to help us learn to communicate respectfully with each other – recognizing the ways in which we are similar and different;
- as a professional relating to a client, to negotiate a safe and suitable therapeutic frame (Gray 1994);
- to offer compassion, protection, permission, empowerment and nurturing for her most vulnerable states, where the abuse and cumulative trauma of neglect and discounting took their toll – to heal the shame;
- to demonstrate respect, interest and engagement in the here and now of our meeting;
- to offer coaching, modelling and advice for her to develop self care to secure her own future and learn always to take good care of her body, mind and soul;
- and finally, to make possible a space for the transpersonal – a connection of spirits as Liza develops a vision of her purpose in life that is big enough to give meaning to all the horrendous experiences she has had.

In spite of all my training and experience, and my best intentions, I can never guarantee we can build a relationship resilient enough to survive the inevitable knocks. Will we cope with the therapeutic crises that will shake us from time to time?

In conclusion, I would work with Liza as I would with anyone, as I would with some other survivors, and as I would with no other individual in the world. In this way I would wish to recognize her uniqueness, her cultural specificity and her universality (Kluckhohn and Murray 1948). While at times we may need to negotiate between conflicting parts of herself, particularly to keep her safe, overall I would tend to emphasize her integrity over her multiplicity. I would not encourage regressive work until much later, when she is functioning well in her present life and our relationship and her sense of who she is appears significantly more robust.

References

Aldridge-Morris, R. (1989) *Multiple Personality: an Exercise in Deception.* London: Erlbaum.

American Psychiatric Association (APA) (1980) *Diagnostic and Statistical Manual of Mental Disorders* (DSM III). Washington, DC: American Psychiatric Association.

American Psychiatric Association (APA) (1994) *Diagnostic and Statistical Manual of Mental Disorders* (DSM IV). Washington, DC: American Psychiatric Association.

Armstrong, L. (1996) *Rocking the Cradle of Sexual Politics: What Happened When Women Said Incest.* London: The Women's Press.

Assagioli, R. (1965) *Psychosynthesis.* London: Mandala.

Balint, M. (1964) *The Doctor, His Patient and the Illness.* London: Pitman.

Barker, N. (1992) *The Prodigy Text: Diagnostic Signs of MPD.* Astraea's Multiple Personality Resources on the World Wide Web.

Berne, E. (1961) *Transactional Analysis in Psychotherapy.* New York: Grove Press.

Clarkson, P. (1992) *Transactional Analysis Psychotherapy.* London: Routledge.

Clarkson, P. (1996) *The Therapeutic Relationship.* London: Whurr.

Cohen, B., Giller, E. and Lynn, W. (eds) (1991) *Multiple Personality Disorder from the Inside Out.* Lutherville, MD: The Sidran Press.

Erskine, R. G. (1997) *Theories and Methods of an Integrative Transactional Analysis.* San Francisco: TA Press.

Foucault, M. (1972) *The Archaeology of Knowledge.* London: Tavistock.

Frank, J. (1973) *Persuasion and Healing: A Comparative Study of Psychotherapy.* Baltimore, MD: Johns Hopkins Press.

Gilbertson, A. *et al.* (1992) Susceptibility of common self-report measures of dissociation to malingering, *Dissociation,* 5: 216–20.

Gray, A. (1994) *An Introduction to the Therapeutic Frame.* London: Routledge.

Hacking, I. (1995) *Rewriting the Soul: Multiple Personality and the Sciences of Memory.* Princeton, NJ: Princeton University Press.

Hocking, Sandra and Company (1992) *Living with Your Selves: A Survival Manual for People with Multiple Personalities.* Rockville, MD: Launch Press.

International Society for the Study of Dissociation (ISSD) (1994) *Guidelines for Treating Dissociative Identity Disorder (Multiple Personality Disorder) in Adults.* Skokie, IL: ISSD.

Janet, P. (1907) *Major Symptoms of Hysteria*. New York: Macmillan.

Kaufman, G. (1989) *The Psychology of Shame*. London: Routledge.

Kepner, J. (1995) *Healing Tasks: Psychotherapy with Adult Survivors of Childhood Abuse*. San Francisco: Gestalt Institute of Cleveland.

Kluckhohn, C. and Murray, H. A. (1948) Personality formation: the determinants, in C. Kluckhohn and H. A. Murray (eds) *Personality in Nature, Society and Culture*. New York: Random House.

Kluft, R. P. (1994) Multiple personality disorder: observations on the etiology, natural history, recognition, and resolution of a long-neglected condition, in R. M. Klein and B. K. Doone (eds) *Psychological Concepts and Dissociative Disorders*. Hillsdale, NJ: Erlbaum.

Kohut, H. (1984) *How Does Analysis Cure?* Chicago: University of Chicago Press.

Kuhn, T. (1962) *The Structure of Scientific Revolutions*. Chicago: University of Chicago Press.

Lago, C. and Thompson, J. (1996) *Race, Culture and Counselling*. Buckingham: Open University Press.

Levitt, E. E. (1988) Questions about multiple personality, *The Harvard Mental Health Letter*, April.

Leys, R. (1992) The real Miss Beauchamp: gender and the subject of imitation, in J. P. Butler and J. W. Scott (eds) *Feminists Theorize the Political*. London: Routledge.

Loftus, E. F. and Ketchum, K. (1994) *The Myth of Repressed Memory: False Memories and Allegations of Sexual Abuse*. New York: St. Martin's.

McGuire, A. (1997) *False Memory Syndrome: A Statement*. Rugby: British Association for Counselling.

Mollon, P. (1996) *Multiple Selves, Multiple Voices: Working with Trauma, Violation and Dissociation*. Chichester: Wiley.

Perls, F. (1992) *Ego Hunger and Aggression*. Highland, NY: The Gestalt Journal Press. (Originally published 1947.)

Polster, E. (1995) *A Population of Selves*. San Francisco: Jossey-Bass.

Putman, F. W. (1993) Diagnosis and clinical phenomenology of multiple personality disorder: a North American perspective, *Dissociation*, 6: 80–6.

Radden, J. (1996) *Divided Minds and Successive Selves: Ethical Issues in Disorders of Identity and Personality*. Cambridge, MA: Massachusetts Institute of Technology.

Rivera, M. (1991) Multiple personality disorder and the social systems: 185 cases, *Dissociation*, 4: 79–82.

Rose, N. (1996) *Inventing Our Selves*. New York: Cambridge University Press.

Rowan, J. (1990) *Subpersonalities*. London: Routledge.

Rowan, J. and Cooper, M. (eds) (1998) *The Plural Self: Multiplicity in Everyday Life*. London: Sage.

Sandler, J. and Freud, A. (1985) *The Analysis of Defence: The Ego and the Mechanisms of Defence Revisited*. New York: International Universities Press.

Schreiber, F. (1973) *Sybil*. Harmondsworth: Penguin.

Sills, C. (ed.) (1997) *Contracts in Counselling*. London: Sage.

Spanos, N. P. (1994) Multiple identity enactments and multiple personality disorder. A sociocognitive perspective, *Psychological Bulletin*, 116: 143–65.

Spiegel, D. (1993) Dissociation and trauma, in D. Spiegel (ed.) *Dissociative Disorders: A Clinical Review*. Lutherville, MD: Sidran Press.

Steiner, C. (1990) *Scripts People Live*. New York: Grove Weidenfeld.

Stern, D. (1985) *The Interpersonal World of the Infant*. New York: Basic Books.

Stuart, L. (1997) How to spot serious regression. (private communication)

Sullivan, H. S. (1953) *The Interpersonal Theory of Psychiatry*. New York: Norton.

Thigpen, C. H. and Cleckley, H. (1957) *The Three Faces of Eve*. New York: McGraw-Hill.
van der Kolk, B. and Fisler, R. (1995) Dissociation and the fragmentary nature of traumatic memories: overview and exploratory study, *Journal of Traumatic Stress*, 8: 505–25.
Walker, M. (1992) *Surviving Secrets*. Buckingham: Open University Press.
Walker, M. (1996) Working with abuse survivors: the recovered memory debate, in R. Bayne, I. Horton and J. Bimrose (eds) *New Directions in Counselling*. London: Routledge.
Warner, M. (1997) A client-centred approach to therapeutic work with dissociated and fragile process. Unpublished paper, Chicago Counseling and Psychotherapy Center.
Woolams, S. and Brown, M. (1978) *Transactional Analysis*. Dexter, MI: Huron Valley Institute Press.

Chapter 6

Multiple personality: an integrative approach

John and Marcia Davis

Introduction

We met and trained as clinical psychologists in the PhD programme at Indiana University in the 1960s, where the Psychological Clinic served both the university and the local community. The training was quite eclectic in orientation, including Rogerian, psychodynamic and Kellian influences. What we now know as cognitive therapy was also exciting interest with the publication of Ellis's *Reason and Emotion in Psychotherapy*, while behaviour therapies were in their infancy and were more in favour in our academic than in our clinical programme. Indeed one of us can recall having to argue strongly with a supervisor to be allowed to try *in vivo* desensitization with a client. Our training also included a one-year internship in San Francisco at the Langley Porter Neuropsychiatric (now Psychiatric) Institute, part of the University of California Medical School. There our eclectic horizons were further widened through influences which included those of Eric Berne, who was resident, Fritz Perls, who offered visiting workshops, and the celebrated Jungian analyst Joseph Wheelwright, who was a regular external contributor to the programme. We were also involved in such diverse enterprises as psychodrama, family therapy and community psychology. Later, these formative experiences were reflected in the MSc course in Psychotherapy that we developed and ran at the University of Warwick from 1978 to 1994 as a post-qualification course, mainly for clinical psychologists. Here we supported trainees in their efforts to develop their own integrative models of practice. Our careers in England over the past 30 years have been National Health Service-based with an academic component (MLD), and academic-based with a clinical NHS component (JDD), both of us centring our clinical work in adult mental health.

During our clinical training, incest was briefly discussed as an extremely rare occurrence unlikely to be encountered in the course of routine clinical practice, although paradoxically it was rumoured to be not so infrequent among the very large isolated families found in the backwoods of Indiana. Kinsey's ground-breaking studies of human sexual behaviour at the Sex Institute on our doorstep had confirmed the supposed rarity of incestuous experience. At Langley Porter there was great interest in a rare case of 'hysterical blindness' in a 17-year-old woman, who disclosed a sexual relationship with her brother during a drug-induced abreaction. However, this constituted the sum total of our training in child sexual abuse when we came to England in 1968. As is well known, a climatic change occurred in the 1970s and the secrecy and denial surrounding the occurrence of child sexual abuse within families began to be dispelled. Suddenly we and other practitioners found many of our adult patients revealing such traumatic histories and so we began to learn something about the effects of such experience and the particular therapeutic issues they give rise to.

In 1978 one of us (JDD) began seeing a young woman who displayed classical borderline features, but presented a picture of a seemingly happy childhood. Only after a considerable time in therapy did this denial begin to break down with the emergence of identified alters in sessions and the gradual disclosure of a severe abuse history. Since there seemed to be no one in Britain who had encountered such cases and since even in the USA a modern literature on dissociation and multiplicity was only just beginning to emerge, this was very much seat-of-the-pants therapy and a valuable education in its own right. Astonishingly it was not long before a second patient turned out to be multiple too. What was JDD doing to induce multiplicity in his patients? In discussions between us, MLD remained somewhat sceptical about the phenomena of multiplicity, but it was not to be long before she was herself treating her first, and soon after a second, multiple patient. Since then we have between us treated a number of patients with dissociative disorders and assessed, consulted with, and supervised work with many more. We have been involved for many years with what is now the International Society for the Study of Dissociation (ISSD) and the Ritual Abuse Information Network and Support (RAINS), while one of us (JDD) has held what is probably the first NHS post to be designated as a speciality in dissociative disorders. We have also conducted research on the prevalence of dissociative disorders which indicates that these disorders, including multiple personality disorder, are relatively common within adult mental health out-patient services in this country, as has also been found in North America. Fortunately, the number of British practitioners who are knowledgeable about dissociative disorders and have experience of treating them is slowly increasing.

Understanding multiplicity

We view multiplicity as a condition that arises in childhood, probably within a critical pre-pubertal period, though its detection (if it is detected at all) occurs only infrequently before adulthood. We take a largely traumatogenic view of the origins of multiplicity based on recourse to dissociation as a defence, or, as we would prefer to term it, a coping resource. We use the term 'dissociation' to refer to any disruption in the usually integrated functions of consciousness, affect, memory, identity, and perception of the external environment. While minor disruptions in mental functions that are usually integrated are a common feature of everyday experience, more extreme and enduring disruptions characterize the dissociative disorders. The main feature of multiplicity is the partitioning of consciousness, together with affect, memory, identity, and perception of the external environment, into segregated states. We note incidentally that the integration of functions referred to above represents a developmental achievement; for example, borderline personality disorder is based not on a disruption of integrated functions, but on a failure to achieve self and object constancy. In our view multiplicity can be overlaid on a personality that is already borderline, or not, depending on the availability of a relatively benign environment in the very early years of development. In this way borderline features will be absent in later-onset multiplicity but are likely to be present where the onset is early.

In the face of stressors, people generally have a repertoire of coping strategies that can be called into play, though they may not always be able to exercise voluntary control over their choices and may or may not be conscious of the coping process. Coping strategies can be broadly divided into those that approach the stressor and those that avoid it. Approach strategies have many advantages for adaptation and adjustment. They enable a person to apprehend the meaning and salience of the stressor; they allow the release of appropriate affect; they provide information about the stressful event that can be used to take remedial action; and they allow the event to be integrated into the person's cognitive-affective schemata of the self and the external world. However, they also involve potential costs. If remedial action is unavailable, the person will experience a sense of vulnerability and helplessness and a heightened level of anxiety; if core features of the person's cognitive-affective schemata are threatened, anxiety will be similarly intensified; and the negative affect aroused by experience of the event may reach an intensity at which the person becomes dysfunctional. In contrast, avoidance strategies minimize the emotional impact of the stressor, so protecting the person from being affectively overwhelmed and enabling the person to experience a sense of control. But they do not allow the person to take remedial action, to release appropriate affect, or to integrate the event into self and world schemata.

Trauma may be thought of as experience of a stressful event in which attempts at coping through approach result in the person being cognitively and affectively overwhelmed. As a result avoidance measures, which may include the defences of denial, dissociation, and repression, are rapidly set in train. Instead of being assimilated, the experience then remains unmetabolized but continues to exert disorganizing effects on the person's behaviour. Freud spoke of the compulsion to repeat the trauma as current reality and to symbolize and master actively what the person was previously overwhelmed by passively. In post-traumatic stress disorder (PTSD) we see a continuing oscillation between these (involuntary) attempts at approach, in the form of intrusive thoughts and images associated with the trauma and revivifications of the experience in dissociative flashbacks and recurrent dreams, and attempts at avoidance, in the form of numbing of affect, social withdrawal, and more generally avoidance of thoughts, feelings, places, people, and activities that might call the trauma to mind. Self-harm and self-medication with alcohol, drugs, or food may also serve such an avoidant function. The tension between approach and avoidance may be reflected in hyperarousal, hypervigilance, insomnia and irritability, as well as in compromise formations such as psychosomatic symptoms that reflect 'body memories' of the trauma.

Such dramatic sequelae can emerge in relatively intact adults as a result of a single traumatic experience that is bounded in time and in which primary attachment figures are not involved. The challenge to the coping resources of a young child experiencing traumas that are repeated incessantly through much of its childhood and which threaten the primary attachments on which its development depends is correspondingly great. We believe that these are the circumstances in which, within a framework of chronic post-traumatic stress disorder, multiplicity typically develops. Dissociation is a coping resource par excellence for survival in an environment where traumatizing experiences are constantly repeated and are inescapable. In particular, the partitioning of consciousness into segregated states permits at least a part of the developing child to experience only the most benign aspects of the environment available and to present the outward appearances of normal development to the casual observer. Intolerable ambivalences can also be avoided by assigning polarized cognitions and affects to different states of consciousness. Functionality can be sustained in the face of affects and cognitions that might otherwise severely impair it (for example suicidal depression) by assigning them to states that are accessed only under very restricted conditions. Similarly, affects and cognitions that might expose the child to danger if expressed or voiced (for example rage) can be assigned to states that are accessed only under conditions of safety. Critically, the partitioning of the experience of trauma reduces it to doses that are survivable, and there is no state of consciousness in which the child appreciates the awesome magnitude of the trauma that is being experienced *in toto*. Even if some states provide an intellectual awareness of the collectivity of trauma, it is never viewed or experienced as a collectivity owned by the self.

There are many unanswered questions about the process of dissociative splitting, and in particular about the process through which alter personalities are created. Disembodiment is a commonly reported experience in the face of physical trauma, with the disembodied self observing the trauma inflicted on the body as if it were happening to someone else. We believe that in the imaginative child this self-hypnotic process is taken a step further by bestowing an identity, and often a name, on the (not-me) self experiencing the trauma. With repetitions of the trauma, the child identifies cues for exiting (dissociating) when a repetition is imminent, leaving the new alter to take over the experience. With the passage of time and repeated interaction with the traumatizing environment, the qualities of the new alter become differentiated and defined and the functions to be served by the alter become more fully delineated. We also believe that as the initial benefits of this process become apparent, the child turns increasingly to dissociation as a recourse in the face of stress, threat or anxiety. Alters then begin to proliferate, not only to deal with whatever varieties of trauma the environment delivers, but also to assume other functions as outlined above, to perform tasks that cause the child anxiety (for example social interactions at school), to preserve capacities that might be put at risk if given open expression, and to assume internal management responsibilities within the growing alter system. Another factor that may govern the cre-ation of new alters is the limited capacity of a single alter to endure trauma without being overwhelmed. We believe that the dissociative process can be repeated by an alter to produce alters that operate at a 'deeper' level (in this sense alters might be viewed as layered). Alternatively, several alters may be created to share responsibility for dealing with a particular aspect of the traumatizing environment. Or again, alters may 'die' or become dormant if overwhelmed and new alters created to take over their functions. The flow of information within the developing system as reflected in the patterning of amnesic barriers and co-consciousness among alters appears to be established on a need-to-know, or more accurately on a need-not-to-know, basis.

We have been frequently struck by the ingenuity displayed in the organization and management of such multiple systems, and it is tempting to posit an inner intelligence or homunculus that designs the system. This would appear to be a paradoxical concept, since it implies a hidden state of consciousness in which many of the mental functions and contents that have been dissociated are actually integrated. If so, where was the need for the original dissociation? Yet we have encountered in one or two instances just such a state, identified in the literature as an inner self-helper (ISH), which does not appear to function as an alter but emerges briefly at points of therapeutic impasse to enlighten the struggling therapist about the system and the impasse that has been reached. Some commentators liken the ISH to the 'hidden observer' identified in some hypnotized individuals, which appears to be aware of the total experience of the individual. We leave the question open.

Understanding Liza

We begin our discussion of Liza by observing that she is not referred to by name in the account we are offered. This suggests that it is Liza who is giving the account in the first person – indeed we are told in the preface that 'she' tells her story herself in a series of interviews. Liza appears to be the host personality in the system, i.e. the one who spends the most time in control of the body and in interaction with the external environment. Most often in clinical settings it is the host who is referred for help and who presents initially in treatment. Often, too, in clinical settings the presenting host is unaware of her multiplicity and of the existence of alters, or is only sketchily aware of their existence and qualities and is frightened by this awareness. Liza presents more as the host might present after some time in therapy, when she has come to accept her multiplicity and has learned a good deal about the system of which she is a part. In Liza's case, this development seems to have come about as much through her self-help efforts as through external facilitation.

Should Liza be viewed as just one alter among many, or is there some intrinsic difference between Liza and the others, 'I' versus 'they'? Is she acting as spokesperson for the system because that is one of her functions, or because the other alters have a secondary status as dissociative epiphenomena? It is often tempting to suppose that the host is the 'original' personality, but in our experience this is not necessarily so. The original or core personality has not infrequently 'died' or become dormant somewhere along the way and the host has been created to take up the reins. We would therefore see it as a mistake to assume that the host is the 'real' person to whom the other alters are appendages.

Working with someone like Liza in a therapeutic context, we would generally anticipate becoming acquainted with the system through encountering and talking with alters directly, not just indirectly through the host. The interviews on which Liza's account is based appear very different in this respect. There is only one point, at the very beginning of the account, at which it seems that an alter might have intervened directly in an interview, though the enigmatic 'somebody else takes over' sounds like a comment by Liza, perhaps on reviewing a taped recording of an interview. One of the limitations of hearing only from Liza is that she can only tell us what she knows. Thus there may be important information about the alters she describes that is omitted, and we do not know how much of the system is as yet quite unknown to her. In a therapeutic context, too, the question of whether there are parts of the system that are still concealed is ever present.

The traumatogenic view of the origins of multiplicity in childhood is well supported by Liza's account. It is important to bear in mind that what Liza is able to report about childhood trauma is bound to be only the tip of an iceberg, since some of her alters will have been created expressly to save her from the experience of trauma and to become repositories for the memories of her traumatic experience. From her opening comments, it seems that coping with physical and emotional abuse was more manageable than coping with sexual abuse and did not require the same dissociative defences. Although we might therefore expect to hear a good deal about Liza's experience of childhood physical abuse as well as emotional abuse, we in fact hear mostly about her *fear* of her father's physical abuse and about her emotional ill-treatment and neglect. The earliest report of physical abuse is found in her account of her father's attempt to strangle Maimie, presumably at the age of 13, but Liza had in fact dissociated and did not experience the violence herself. In later adolescent and adult relationships, particularly her first marriage, there appears to have been a good deal of physical abuse, but again it seems to be alters rather than Liza who experience it. We therefore wonder whether she has childhood memories of physical abuse that are not described, or perhaps remembers more the pervasive threat of physical violence should she step out of line. She has sufficient memory fragments to know from her 'own' experience that sexual abuse took place, and reports recently 're-owning' the early memory of being raped by her father held by 4-year-old Billy. We also recognize the possibility that some of her memory fragments represent part-episodes up to the point of switching to a designated alter. Suffice it to say that she would appear from an early age to have experienced direct sexual and emotional abuse as well as severe neglect at the hands of a primary attachment figure, her father, together with her mother's effective complicity in the neglect and failure to protect her from the abuse. The failure to protect seems to have extended to other experiences of sexual abuse outside the family, memories of which are held by other alters such as Joan and Nadia.

Liza, the host, appears to be the personality that enjoyed the best – or, rather, the least pernicious – aspects of the traumatizing environment in which the system of alters developed. In families such as Liza's, the host is typically enmeshed in the external family system, while the drive to separate and individuate is represented elsewhere in the internal system of alters (for example Dudley's dislike of families and her leaving home). As the dissociation begins to break down, what Liza as host experiences is the conflict between preservation of the external family system ('you can go with your mum and dad and side with them') and disengagement from it ('you can believe the rape and you've got to do something about it; you've got to stick up for her and for the others'). Thus we see that multiplicity (which is not infrequently generational in families) also serves homeostatic functions for the external family system. We would imagine that it is Liza as host who is most involved in the ongoing relationship with her parents, though we would also be alert to the possibility that the sexual relationship with the father may continue, unknown to her, through the agency of other alters.

Some points about the system of alters (as Liza is able to describe it) merit comment. The variation in age, gender, and sexual orientation is typical within such systems. What is less common is the continuing creation of new alters at the age of 29. We are told of at least three alters being created within the last three years: Sparkie, whose initial function may have been to escape from an abusive marital relationship; the unnamed alter who goes to the sexual abuse project, whose initial function may have been to cope with the bereavement on Jason's death; and the unnamed psychology student, whose principal function may have been to try marriage on a new footing. Ordinarily, the need to create new alters diminishes with increasing age because the traumatizing environment has been left behind. What we see here, with Sparkie, is remedial but anxiety-laden action to deal with a new traumatizing environment, action that is presumably too daunting for Liza to undertake. The second alter appears to be designed to cope with a new trauma, bereavement, where no remedial action is possible. The third alter's function seems to be to take a developmental step forward that also engenders considerable anxiety. These recent dissociative solutions to problems bear out how pervasive is the tendency to fall back on dissociation as a resource, even in situations that could not be deemed traumatic.

At the other end of the age spectrum we have an alter aged 6 months. The concept of such a young alter poses several questions. How does Liza know that its age is 6 months, given that the alter will have no language to proclaim its own age? Was the alter created when Liza was 6 months old? Can experiences at the age of 6 months be encoded and retrieved later in life? Traditional cognitive-developmental psychology tells us that this is impossible, though recent research has suggested that retrievable memory can be laid down at a much earlier age than was formerly suspected. We do not know the answer to these questions, although we doubt that cognitive development would permit the creation of an alter at that age. Nevertheless, it is certainly not uncommon to find infant alters in multiple systems, and we would note that an alter's 'age' does not have to correspond to the chronological age at which the alter came into being, even if such correspondence is in most cases a natural feature of the creative process. For example, we have encountered elderly alters in young adult patients.

Equally, the gender of an alter does not have to correspond to biological gender and it is common to find alters of the opposing gender. In Liza's case, she says that she thinks Mands is a boy, though she continually refers to him as 'she'. Later she says she thinks there is one male personality, but he has yet to make himself known. Liza as host seems somewhat uncertain as to whether she has male alters, and there is nothing in her account of Mands to indicate what function a male gender might serve. In other contexts

maleness might be associated with the strength to repel unwanted atten-
tions, with a wish to intimidate, with a wish to escape sexual attention by not
being a girl, or with a wish to secure parental (usually maternal) love by being
of the parentally desired gender.

At least two alters, Maimie and Dudley, assume the ambivalence
about sexual orientation that is commonly found following protracted childhood sexual abuse, leaving Liza with an uncomplicated heterosexual orientation. Maimie is described as bisexual, but no account of any sexual
relationships is given. Dudley is described as 'gay or bisexual', but all the relationships referred to are homosexual and it sounds as though she experiences
sexual attention from men as threatening and tries to avoid it. She is said to
have left home and started a new life on the gay scene that lasted 'a few' years
and to have lived with a woman for 'a couple' of years, but there is no indication of Liza's status as host during this period – whether she was responsible
at that time for managing most interactions with the external environment
and whether she was oblivious to the gay scene and Dudley's homosexual
relationships. Although Dudley is described as 'punky' and 'aggressive', she is
the one who ends up getting hit by her partners and abused in her two-year
relationship.

We can also see in Liza's account a variety of features of the alter system
that fit our earlier theoretical discussion. A number of alters (for example
Billie, Nadia, Joan, Mrs B) seem to have been designed initially to cope with
trauma and to hold the memories of trauma. While Liza as host is always anxious to please, other alters (for example Tracey, Mands) hold the anger she
feels it would be dangerous to express. While Liza is at times self-punitive,
some of these feelings are assigned to other alters (for example Mands, 'Spot')
and Liza fears that there may be a more suicidal alter in the system. A number
of alters preserve talents or abilities that are not currently available to Liza (for
example Godspell, Joan, Armada, the college student, the choirgirl). Others
have specialist responsibilities for handling pregnancy and/or childbirth (for
example Maimie, Joan), managing sexual encounters (for example Tracey, the
sexy-seductive husband-catcher), and possibly pursuing self-understanding
and healing (Sparkie and the two newest alters). System management functions seem to be shared among several alters (for example Joan, Armada, the
alter that keeps others quiet, the alter that seeks to stop Liza dissociating). We
also learn in the account that certain alters were intended to 'take over' from
others (for example Tracey from Mands, Armada from Joan). It is also note-
worthy that some alters have multiple functions. Joan, in particular, seems to
carry an extremely heavy workload. She seems to have been created to endure
the sexual abuse associated with mother's workplace and to hold the associated memories, but she has also acquired responsibilities for looking after the
younger child alters and keeping them quiet, for holding talents for musical
performance, poetry writing, and making things, as well as for managing
pregnancies and childbirth – and all this at the tender age of 10. It is unclear

why some alters should be so burdened, when it would seem as easy to create new alters to meet new responsibilities, but within all the systems we have encountered a small number of alters typically play pivotal roles.

It seems from Liza's account that there is a good deal of co-consciousness in the system and that host–alter boundaries are relatively permeable. She says that she sees Tracey as separate from herself, but is not sure about the others – sometimes they are separate and sometimes they are not. Her consciousness is often continuous even when she believes that another alter has taken over, and she is then not amnesic for the experience. For example, talking about her pregnancies, she wonders if 'a different self takes over and is more in the body', but the experience remains her own and she is at her happiest then. Or again, when unable to open the front door 'all the old feelings came up', but she understands these as belonging to a child alter who feels trapped. In contrast, there are other occasions when she can go into a toilet and lose time, becoming amnesic for what she believes is experienced by the same child alter in the interim. We believe this illustrates what she means by saying that sometimes they are separate and sometimes not. When the boundary becomes permeable, it is hard for Liza to distinguish between herself and the alter, and in her account she may switch between first and third person. For example, in discussing Mands she speaks of 'things *I* remember about Mands', 'him [dad] making sexual comments about *me*', and 'him [boyfriend] trying things on with *her*'. Similarly, it is Liza who writes the alters' journals – 'As soon as *I*'ve written everything down that *they* wanted to write . . .'.

It is difficult to be sure whether this degree of co-consciousness is a relatively new development for Liza, although it is tempting to imagine that it has coincided with the gradual return of dissociated memories and represents a dilution of amnesic barriers. Paradoxically, however, it is only over the last two years that she is aware of losing time, whereas she might be expected to have lost much more time if co-consciousness had been more limited in the past. It appears that this question is the subject of disagreement within the system. One possibility is that being more continuously 'present' has sensitized her to her 'absences', whereas previously she took them in her stride as part of her normal experience. Referring to apparent time loss and subsequent spatial disorientation, she says that she used to be able to cope with it – 'you don't know what it is and you just cope with it, it's normal to you'. She reports one such 'absence' (lasting a couple of days) several years ago, which seems to have taken her attention primarily because of what her friend Jason told her she had been doing in the interim (sleeping with a man she had picked up), and goes on to suggest that there may have been hundreds of such instances. She also disclaims all knowledge of getting up in the night to feed her first child (ten years ago), although it was clear to her at the time that the feeding was taking place. And of course the process of retrieving memories is a strong indication to her that she did not always enjoy the levels of co-consciousness that she currently enjoys and that, unless she subsequently 'forgot' her experiences, she must have been 'absent' and lost time when they occurred.

Liza's account of the ongoing effects of her abuse includes some features that are common in people with histories of severe childhood sexual abuse but are not particularly linked to her multiplicity: for example feeling dirty and bathing a lot, depending on alcohol, self-mutilation, repeating abusive relationships, not knowing how to set boundaries as a parent. Others resemble chronic PTSD symptoms, for example shaking and living on the edge, nightmares. More linked to her dissociation are body memories/psychosomatic symptoms, phobias, and the panic attacks brought on by the imminent breakdown of amnesic barriers. The intermittent quality of her anorexia seems more directly linked to her multiplicity, and perhaps reflects the intermittent influence/presence of her anorexic alter, Dudley.

We conclude our discussion of Liza with one or two brief comments. First, regarding Liza's belief that Tracey may have 'died' following Jason's death, we referred earlier to the possibility of alters 'dying' if cognitively and affectively overwhelmed, but it is not clear why Tracey would have suffered this fate, particularly as it is Joan who is charged with dealing with deaths. In our experience it is usually possible to 'resurrect' dead alters in therapy. Secondly, the individual medical histories for alters provide an interesting record. We presume that when examining Liza's medical records, alters would convey their own contributions to the records, but we would like to hear more about the process of identification. On a slightly different note, we have experience of patients well into therapy bringing collections of photographs from childhood and adolescence and identifying alters with little hesitation. We have also had some success in making blind identifications which match these attributions. Finally, Liza's account of living with different selves conveys well the kinds of conflict and difficulty that attend multiplicity, from the minor aspects of everyday life to occupational choice and the development and maintenance of relationships. In fact, for all the difficulties that she experiences, we would say that Liza's system shows a healthy degree of cooperation and collaboration in this respect. Even in the past when the alters were more inclined simply to do their own thing, there appeared to be little mutual antagonism or warfare within the system. We have seen patients whose systems of alters have displayed much more internal conflict, marked by external acts of hostility or sabotage. For example, one college student alter would find that her assignments were being destroyed before she could submit them for assessment. The closest approach to such behaviour that we hear about in Liza's account is when Mands picks at her (Liza's) skin to stop her wearing nice clothes (and possibly to make her unattractive to her husband).

Therapeutic intervention and difficulties

Our approach to helping a patient with a similar history and presentation to Liza's would depend somewhat on her (or his) current status at the time of seeking help. Liza herself has already made considerable progress towards achieving some of the sub-goals we would need to pursue with a patient who was starting 'further back'. For present purposes we will assume that the presenting host is largely ignorant of the existence of her alters, or has experienced them only as voices in her head, and has no knowledge of dissociative disorders. She is probably aware that her memory is very bad, so bad in fact that there are periods of time she cannot account for, so bad that she sometimes does not know where she is or sometimes does not know people who evidently know her. However, her ticket of admission is likely to be one or more of the multifarious problems that are likely to accompany multiplicity. Liza, for example, could have presented with panic attacks/agoraphobia, anorexia, compulsive self-mutilation, phobia, psychosomatic complaints, or relationship problems among others. She is not likely to volunteer the experiences that make her think she must be mad.

We believe that with our current degree of experience, we are likely to pick up enough clues in initial consultation to tell us that we may be dealing with a dissociative disorder. At this point, one of us (MLD) would introduce formal assessment tools, including a dissociative experiences questionnaire and an interview schedule for dissociative disorders. The purpose is less for diagnostic assessment than to universalize for the patient her dissociative experiences – to allow her to feel that she is not alone with them, that there are others with similar experiences, and that there are professional helpers who understand them. The groundwork is also laid for what may be a protracted process of accepting and coming to terms with her multiplicity. The other (JDD) prefers not to use formal assessment devices in this way, but pursues similar objectives at a slower pace following material that emerges spontaneously in therapeutic sessions.

Both of us, as in any therapy, attach great importance to fostering, nourishing and keeping in as good repair as possible the therapeutic working alliance. This is a challenge when working with somebody whose trust has been betrayed by primary attachment figures, and the therapist's reliability will be tested severely and repeatedly over the course of therapy in the confident expectation that trust will be betrayed and abused. The more reliable the therapist appears to be, the more frightening the patient's investment in the therapeutic relationship becomes and the more there is to be lost if trust is placed in the therapist. It is common in the early stages of therapy for some alters to be opposed to the enterprise, to warn against it internally, and possibly to try and sabotage it. Part of the therapist's reliability initially consists in setting clear boundaries and contractual understandings and sticking to them. We think that the clarity and reliability are often more critical than the details, such as frequency and duration of sessions, so long as these are consensually agreed. But in negotiating the details, it is also important for the therapist to anticipate what might be required later on (as we will discuss below). Another important aspect of establishing a good alliance is the negotiation of therapeutic goals and ways of working towards them. Initially, before the patient understands what is wrong with her, it is not possible to consider what the long-term goals might be, and we would work with the immediate objectives expressed by the patient, for example some sort of symptomatic relief. However, we would propose to her that an initial sub-goal would be to try and understand why she is experiencing the particular problem(s) she presents. At a later date, as the patient begins to comprehend and accept her multiplicity, it becomes possible to renegotiate the goals to be worked towards and the means of arriving at them. Another difficulty at the beginning is that the patient typically feels that things could not be worse than they are; consequently it is hard to convey in any meaningful way how painful the course of therapy may be and how long it may require, since the patient does not understand what the therapy will entail. None the less, we think that it is important to convey the idea that therapy may need to be long-term and may require substantial courage and fortitude. For the listening alters this will also indicate the therapist's preparedness to make a long-term commitment.

We see the therapy as guided by two major aims. One is to work towards developing and strengthening the coping skills of the host, so that she becomes progressively less reliant on dissociation in dealing with the stresses and strains of daily life. The second is, as in PTSD, to enable her to face and successfully metabolize the traumas that originally led her to dissociate. To the extent that she can do this, many of her handicapping symptoms will become easily resolvable. For example, Liza's phobic response to locking a toilet door is likely linked to a traumatizing experience in which being locked in a toilet constituted at least one element. Weakening the dissociative barriers between the patient and her alters makes the traumatic memories they hold increasingly accessible to her to the point of abreaction, when she can be helped to process the trauma cognitively and affectively and own it as hers. Such work needs to be carefully managed so that a sense of safety is preserved and she is able to reorientate herself in time and place before leaving sessions. Weakening the dissociative barriers within the system implies seeking at every turn to increase the flow of information between host and alters and among the alters, seeking to persuade them of their connectedness, and convincing them that they share the same body. Success in these endeavours also does much to facilitate internal democracy, recognition of mutual needs and rights, and collaborative functioning in managing the external environment. The means of fostering intra-system communication rest with the combined wit and ingenuity of therapist and patient – Liza, for example, has devised useful tools in her models of the alters and the alters' journals.

The work of confronting traumas that overwhelmed the patient earlier in her life is inevitably very frightening, painful, and taxing, as Liza's account bears out, but other realizations that develop in the course of therapy can also be exceedingly painful and bring the patient to the edge of despair – for example, beginning to appreciate fully the awfulness of her childhood or facing behaviour of her own that she sees as shameful or unforgivable. In anticipation of these difficulties, it is important to establish at an early stage what external supports are available to her, and if these are minimal, to see what, if anything, can be put in place. (Again, resourcefulness may be required – for example, the Internet now provides specialized sites where patients can join support networks for people with dissociative disorders.) Equally, as therapists we need to consider carefully, when establishing or revising the therapeutic frame, to what extent we should make ourselves available between sessions and in what circumstances, taking into account what other supports are available. The prime considerations here are the patient's need to experience a sufficient degree of safety and security to undertake the therapeutic work, and our own need to work within our capacity. Where there is no meeting point, the therapy is unlikely to prosper.

We see it as critical in the process of loosening dissociative barriers for the system of alters to become known to the therapist, to the host, and to one another. Mapping and understanding the alter system is an ongoing part of therapy. In our experience alters often, in the first instance, emerge spontaneously in therapy. Sometimes, they may have been referred to by another alter and emerge in response to the therapist's invitation. Sometimes, they may first come forward in response to a general invitation (for example 'Is there anyone who can throw light on this?') or a specific query (for example 'Who spent the money?'). We see it as our task to engage all the alters in the system and establish multiple working alliances with them. Of particular importance in this regard is the task of engaging alters who are hostile to the therapist and/or the therapy, alters who persecute or punish the host and/or other alters, alters who are violent or perpetrate abuse, alters who are suicidal, and alters who play pivotal roles within the system. Some of the most difficult challenges in this regard arise with alters who are identified with and loyal to the external family members or other external system responsible for the traumas inflicted on the patient. We also see it as important not to collude with the internal system by mirroring group condemnation of a particular alter or group fear of an alter. We defend alters by maintaining that each one came to help the patient in some way and continues to act in ways that he or she believes are in the patient's best interests, even if, because of changing circumstances, that is no longer the case and the alter now needs to learn to help in a different way.

The question of knowing when the mapping of the system is complete is a difficult one, and in our experience it is always possible that undiscovered alters and their attendant traumas and issues can emerge just when patient and therapist believe that this stage of therapy is almost at an end. We believe that there is an internal hierarchy of experiences based on how hard they are to assimilate, with items lowest on the hierarchy coming forward first and items that are highest coming forward last. For example, sexual abuse by fathers seems easier to assimilate than sexual abuse by mothers, and alters who hold memories of maternal abuse may be slower to emerge. Alters who experienced pleasure during such abuse are often held back, while those that hold memories of pain and feelings of anger or disgust appear earlier. Child alters with memories of incestuous abuse are quicker to appear than corresponding adolescent or adult alters. Traumas that involve more horror and terror emerge after more 'benign' traumas, if we can be excused the term. Alters who have, uncoerced, perpetrated abuse on others are late to appear in therapy.

Once the patient has fully accepted her multiplicity and has come to know her alters, when the system of alters is functioning collaboratively, and when the host is making progress in developing her own coping skills, is facing and assimilating her traumatic experiences, and is beginning to get a narrative picture of her past life, it is time to discuss what final therapeutic goals she wishes to pursue. This is essentially a question of whether she wants to maintain her multiplicity or pursue the goal of integration. Often a decision to seek integration is based on a wish to be like other people and not to feel different, since it is impossible for the patient to appreciate what it will feel like not to be multiple (just as it is hard for a person who is integrated to understand what it would feel like to be multiple). Another factor may be a wish to gratify the therapist by achieving the outcome that the therapist is perceived as secretly desiring. This is not a decision that the host can take by herself, since each of the alters will have a view about it, and there may be a lengthy process of discussion and negotiation in which the implications of integration are considered and the fears and aspirations of the different selves are explored. The principal anxiety expressed by alters is often a fear of death and oblivion, although we have not encountered a host expressing such a fear.

Following a decision to remain multiple, therapy will draw to a close once the ongoing work is completed. Following integration substantial therapeutic work remains, though the formal process of integration is easily accomplished through suggestion or autosuggestion, just as we have proposed autosuggestion as the process through which alters are created. There is a frightening sense of aloneness in the newly integrated patient, of having nobody to turn to. The sense of loss is enormous and the patient needs to grieve for the alters and the internal world that have been lost; for the loss of childhood and adolescence, which are experienced in a new way; and for the loss of significant relationships, including her multiple relationships with the therapist, since she is now different and people are different with her. She needs help in learning to tolerate and cope with ambivalence, in renegotiating and redefining her significant relationships, and in facing the daunting responsibility of having to cope with whatever arises. She needs to adjust to the inefficiency of being unitary, since her continuous presence results in her getting tired and feelings that arise in one situation linger on to impair her functioning in the next. And she needs help in reconstructing her own history in a way that has some temporal continuity.

Conclusion

We would like to express our appreciation to Liza for sharing her account with us and allowing us to comment on it. There is also one area we have not discussed, though we think that it is critically important in many cases. As in any therapy, attention needs to be given to the patient's current life space and significant relationships. This is particularly important where the patient has children, when we would want to review with her their safety and consider with her whether there are educational resources and parent groups where she could secure guidance on child-rearing issues. Similarly, it is often helpful if spouses can find support groups for those married to people with dissociative disorders – unfortunately a rare resource in Britain.

Chapter 7

Multiple personality: a personal perspective

Jenifer Antony-Black

Introduction

To consider how I would understand and work with this client (and indeed other women with multiple personality) I need to place this in the context of my own history and experiences. These have formed me both as a person and a counsellor. My first starting point as a counsellor comes from my experience of abuse throughout childhood, followed by a different type of abuse within the psychiatric system. It comes from the development of my ability to dissociate, along with the development of multiple personality. I know what it is like to live with this on a daily basis, although like everyone else, I have had many other life experiences. My second starting point comes from returning to education and gaining qualifications in counselling. Who I am and what I am cannot be separated from how we got there. The way I work with multiple personality is interwoven with the fact that I too have many different selves. This is crucial and central to my way of working.

In view of this my starting point in this chapter is to explain this context of my life and work to the reader – essentially all else follows from this. I will consider some of the specific issues that might arise for counsellors and therapists who like myself are multiple personality. I note here that for the purposes of this chapter I use the terms 'therapist' and 'counsellor' interchangeably. I shall explore traditional approaches within medicine and psychiatry towards multiple personality and will then describe my own therapeutic style and stance. Finally I will specifically look at how I might work with Liza.

I do not wish to suggest that I fully understand multiple personality – there are times when I do not. Neither am I saying that just because I know what it is like to live with, that I can somehow work better with it than other counsellors. Similarly, it is debatable if people who have been abused make the best counsellors. Experience of abuse in itself is far from sufficient to make a person a good counsellor: theoretical knowledge, counselling practice and good supervision are clearly essential, although the counsellor should not get lost in the theory – theory and jargon can obliterate the client's contribution (Jacobs 1988).

As a child I was physically and psychologically abused and sexual abuse followed. Like many abused women I have little memory of childhood. I married as soon as I could to escape the situation. Within a year I was in psychiatric hospital. The following 16 years were spent within the psychiatric system. Diagnosis and treatments changed over the years and included schizophrenia, personality disorder and psychopathic tendencies. Treatments were ECT, anti-depressants and tranquillizers. All the diagnoses were incorrect. Abuse and the long-term effects were never acknowledged. Unfortunately tranquillizers and anti-depressants are still used (Walker 1993) instead of exploring what may be wrong. Listening can prove time consuming and threatening for the medical profession. This treatment changed when I went into a psychotherapy unit: medication ceased, and for the first time I was given the opportunity to talk. Although I was able to say that I had been abused, the long-term effects were still not acknowledged. How I felt, particularly in terms of the dissociation I experienced, was not recognized. Instead I was accused of 'acting out'. On reflection, I now understand that I then created a new self that would be acceptable to society and who would control the other selves. This control was based on fear. We were never going to return to hospital again. This personality learnt to live in the community. She is a 'forgiving' and 'caring' person. Looking back, I recognize that throughout life we were all treated as 'bad' and 'worthless', reinforced in the therapeutic unit where our behaviour was seen as 'bad'. The self who took over therefore needed to be 'good' – that is, to have no unacceptable feelings such as hatred, anger, resentment, and the need for revenge. The list is endless.

I did not know there was a name for my different selves until I entered therapy, although they were familiar before I went into a psychiatric hospital. No one asked if the voices I heard were outside or inside; no one listened or tried to make sense of my experiences. So I learnt to repress everything. My therapist was the first to recognize that I had many selves. We started to tape sessions, solving the problem of my 'losing' them – I would have no recall of what had been discussed. It felt both weird and frightening when I heard the tapes although it made sense of many things. It was like putting a jigsaw into place but not liking the picture. I still have many blank years throughout our/my lives. There are still memories that I have not got. The label 'multiple personality' was initially frightening – dire consequences had resulted from previous psychiatric labels. This earlier mis-diagnosis is illustrated by Bloom, who now works with abuse and with multiple personality:

> Ten years ago if a patient had come to me and told me that he or she had been sexually and physically abused in a satanic cult, and that this person had been forced to engage in the most degrading acts, participating in the sacrifice and cannibalism of infants and adults, I would probably have diagnosed such a person as suffering from some form of paranoid disorder and I would have tried anti-psychotic medication in order to treat the delusions. I would have labelled such dissociative experiences as psychotic.
>
> (Bloom 1994: 287)

As well as my own therapy, training as a counsellor was a vital step forward. I have a diploma in psychodynamic counselling and have also undertaken further training in psychodynamic supervision. This taught me theory while also helping me to understand myself and to place myself in my world and in the wider world. It helped me accept myself as valid, enabling me to know and accept the various personalities rather than seeing them as enemies. Feeling valued at this time gave me strength to allow the others in. Getting to know the other selves was painful because of their memories. I was no longer surprised that the original self had split.

I now work in the Quetzal Project in Leicester, which I set up in 1989. It is a service for women who have been sexually abused as children; and who as a result are experiencing difficulties in their later life, that may include symptoms of mental distress such as anxiety, panic attacks, and depression. It is an independent voluntary organization funded from a variety of sources. The aims of the project are to help women to become more able to deal with the effects of abuse by regaining their self-esteem; to feel more in control; and to understand and manage difficulties in relationships. I developed Quetzal because of a lack of services for adult women experiencing the long-term effects of abuse that were beginning to be recorded at that time (Wyatt and Powell 1988). I wanted others to have the services that I believe would have kept me out of the psychiatric system. I wanted a project where women were believed, and listened to without fear of judgement; a project that provided a choice of services – individual counselling, group work or crisis intervention – recognizing that it is often at times of crisis that women are admitted to hospital.

What is multiple personality?

A good starting point for a counsellor who has not worked with multiple personality is to be honest and say so. The counsellor should ask the client about their experiences instead of pretending that they know. Clients appreciate honesty from the beginning. It is good to remember that in all this work there is a starting point and a first time for working with anything.

The counsellor needs to recognize and accept that within one body there is a group of individual personalities. My experience of working with multiple personality is that these are people who tend to be naturally very creative, often artistic in some way, and more able to create fantasy worlds. Multiple personality can be understood as a very creative response. Perhaps only some truly imaginative children can achieve this response to abuse. Some children are creative, imaginative, very able to enter the worlds and feelings of others, and have very rich make-believe play, including imaginary friends. For those children who are not abused, this creativity may lead them into becoming artistic and creative adults; but perhaps it is this group who have the capacity, if abused, to develop multiple personalities.

For both the counsellor and the client multiple personality can appear chaotic, contradictory and controlling. It is an effective and creative defence mechanism. To understand it we have to recognize that sexual abuse is a horrific experience for a child and that for those systematically abused over a long period of time, one way of surviving is to dissociate. Dissociation is when the mind and body separate – it is like standing outside yourself. In some cases split-off feelings, thoughts and emotions can develop into separate personalities and multiple personalities result. These personalities contain and hold the feelings, thoughts and emotions surrounding the events taking place at that time. The objective of this unconscious strategy is to minimize the impact of what has happened.

The original self is the first to develop following birth. As a response to trauma this self can become void of feelings. When this self is present it is experienced as the 'dead' times. 'I feel dead' is a common statement made by clients with multiple personality. However it is important to note that medication and depression can also create similar feelings. When clients experience these dead times they are extremely hard to work with, since no thought process is present.

Someone with multiple personality experiences having many different voices within. Each voice belongs to a separate autonomous personality with its own thoughts, feelings, emotions and memories. There are selves who serve one purpose, to do a specific job, for instance cleaning. These selves appear to have little awareness once they have completed the task. They do not grow as other personalities can. There can be a 'fun personality'. For the abused child fun times are spoilt, due to the constant fear of further abuse taking place. The 'fun self' protects the good times by separating them off so they do not get spoiled by the bad times. 'Controlling personalities' have the role of silencing everyone: such a personality believes that no one listens anyway, and that punishment may well follow disclosure of any kind. 'Destructive personalities' can believe that they are to blame, feel dirty and blame themselves. This loathing can lead to various forms of self-harm. 'Parental personalities' look after the younger 'selves', and because of difficulties in trusting can prevent the child personalities speaking for themselves. Parental personalities need to learn that hiding child selves away keeps them in a painful haze, and may not be helpful to them. Essentially different selves keep different experiences separate, to manage them or to protect them.

A woman who experiences multiple personalities may have both male and female personalities. The creation of a male self can be due to the need for a physically stronger self; for example, a young female child self who is being bullied can develop a male self to cope with the bullying and to stop it. It is not uncommon for a male self to stereotype women. If a male self is contemptuous of women, this would be present with me as the counsellor and I would need to help that self deal with his hatred of women. Working with a male counsellor who is respectful of women and who does not stereotype can be beneficial. A personality who is refusing to see the value of the opposite sex is devaluing parts of her or himself. Each personality needs to accept the female/male within them. I understand male selves as arising from the introjection/internalization of the abusive father, who then gets projected outwards. Helping clients to understand this can help put some pieces together for them. However, more positive male selves can be present, reflecting that personalities can arise in response both to what has happened, and to what was absent but needed.

There are selves who hold on to the past and hide the memories that can prevent the autonomous selves from functioning. When being counselled, a client with multiple personality may unconsciously switch from one personality to another – a different one comes in to help. This can happen if the feelings engendered in the session become intolerable – remembering that the reason for the splitting in the first place was an unconscious attempt to escape the situation, because of the intolerable pain. This can take place if the counsellor says something that triggers a memory. Switching disrupts life and the counselling process – for example, the self who takes over may not know their surroundings or the people present. They are still in their past. This self may either give information or be silent. And the counsellor can be seen as the abuser.

There are issues of power with and between the different selves. For instance, they compete with each other, fearing that another will gain complete control. This would mean they would no longer be needed. Different personalities react both physically and psychologically against how much time each has. These reactions often determine the effects of multiple personality on daily life.

Traditional responses to multiple personality: denial and complicity

The question should no longer be whether multiple personality exists, rather how we can learn about and understand it. Many women with multiple personalities with whom I work have been through the same psychiatric system as I have. Medical responses to revelations of abuse, in particular where the resulting effects are misunderstood as madness (frequently the case with multiple personality), are often painfully inadequate and entirely inappropriate. Ignorance, fear, and a sense of inadequacy can result in treatment that helps the doctor to feel in control, safe and reassured, rather than listening, understanding and responding helpfully to the patient. The effect of this is to silence women. Drugs can silence the selves who are trying to say something. This appears to be the intent, either consciously or unconsciously: to silence people.

The denial of the reality of multiple personality by the psychiatric and medical professions cannot be seen in isolation. It is part of a wider pattern of denial that is particularly evident with abuse, although also in evidence in respect of other controversial presentations (Gulf War Syndrome is one example.) The medical profession has shown a consistent ability to deny difficult and threatening truths. For example, for a long time baby battering did not exist, and childhood sexual abuse was a fantasy. Denial has a long history. As far back as the nineteenth century Tardieu exposed and detailed both sexual abuse and physical cruelty towards children: 'He had discovered and described what was to be acknowledged a hundred years later as the battered child syndrome' (Summit 1988: 46). In spite of Tardieu's eminence and his great influence on other areas of forensic medicine, his assertions about physical and sexual abuse of children were neglected and ignored. In the late nineteenth century Freud (1896) presented his paper 'The aetiology of hysteria' (Freud 1991) to members of the Vienna Psycho-Analytical Society where he said: 'Almost all my women patients told me that they had been seduced by their fathers' (1991: 54).

Freud later revised his ideas and accepted the additional explanation of phantasy, as he could not accept that actual abuse could be the cause of all hysteria. However, he did not retract completely and his work includes many references to actual abuse in later case studies. In 1932 Ferenczi attempted to convince the psychoanalytic world of the reality of child sexual abuse by the presentation of his paper 'Confusion of tongues between adults and children'. Freud's and Ferenczi's recognition of actual abuse was not widely or actively acknowledged.

Eventually the medical profession acknowledged these realities, often adding the word 'disorder' – implying an illness that only doctors can cure, with consequent medically and/or psychiatrically decided treatments. Thus doctors have reframed and claimed as within their own province something they previously denied, effectively excluding, minimizing or invalidating the legitimate contributions made by others in the care professions, the voluntary sector, and by those who experience the 'disorders'. Most then conveniently forget the past disbelief and dismissiveness of their profession, and the damage this did to people throughout that long period of denial. This pattern is particularly evident with multiple personality.

The effects of ignorance, fear, inadequacies and distorted beliefs give the medical profession and psychiatry the freedom to continue the denial process. This leaves many women with multiple personality trapped and feeling worthless; labelled as liars, or as mad or mentally ill. This happened to me and to many others. Years of life can be destroyed. Patients and their feelings are controlled, rather than their feelings and issues being explored, and a different cycle of abuse can begin. The awfulness of the childhood abuse is perpetuated and accepted in institutionalized abuse in adulthood. These are the reasons why I developed the Quetzal Project. At that time in my life I was driven by rage.

Unfortunately it seems that psychiatry must adopt and accept multiple personality before women can be listened to. What is a psychological defence against an appalling physical and psychological onslaught becomes an illness. The psychiatrist who treated me 20 years ago stated when I saw him again in 1989 that he 'could not believe how ignorant they were then where sexual abuse was concerned'. Psychiatry has no expectations of clients other than that they 'behave'. This means taking medication without explanation, discussion or negotiation, and not asking questions. Psychiatry can be patronizing; and psychiatrists' inability appropriately to challenge or confront not only means their patients are badly treated, but can also result in workers being abused. In an atmosphere that is insufficiently contained abused clients can themselves be abusive as a retaliation for the treatment they have received as children and as adults. Containment via drugs states that a person does not have a right to feelings, let alone to express them.

How I work with multiple personality

As a counsellor I never myself have the goal of integration: that desire has to come from the person, and it might not. Such an aim can be over-emphasized, often reflecting the agenda of the therapist rather than the client. If I am working with a client who wishes to integrate, I consult with colleagues and talk with someone who feels they have gone through this process. In this situation I would need to refer the client to another therapist: I cannot help a client to achieve integration when I do not believe this is necessary.

I have developed my own style of counselling. My own experience of psychotherapy and of being on the receiving end of the psychiatric profession has played a powerful role in shaping me into the kind of counsellor I am. I try to help clients *know* their selves rather than *fear* them – which is what they often feel. They fear being seen as mad. They fear not being believed and not being understood. I work with the client towards achieving a good enough harmony between the selves. My role is to help them to get to know one another and myself, before we can begin to work with them. This process of working with the client to acknowledge their different selves is a painful process. It involves reclaiming the memories that caused the splits in the first place: the experiences were too much for the one person to cope with, and in reclaiming memories they can feel overwhelming all over again. Time and careful pacing are essential.

It is essential to work with all the personalities. Some, notably the destructive ones, may not be very cooperative, but they have to be worked and reasoned with. It must be recognized that all the personalities have a function, and must be heard and respected. With some, especially the aggressive selves, the work has to move towards a point where patterns of behaviour actually and actively have to be changed. This is complex: one aspect is recognizing that such behaviour is based on distorted beliefs. However, it is not enough simply to focus on these beliefs: the reasons for and the meanings of the resulting behaviour have to be understood. Working with underlying conflicts is central.

I draw on two theoretical bases, the psychodynamic and the cognitive. Insight alone is not enough. For example, if a destructive personality is to be helped, that personality needs to face and place the guilt, blame, badness and dirtiness experienced, and the resulting harm to self or others that so often characterizes such a personality. That personality needs to understand the source of this to begin to feel better about themselves and to be valued in their own right. However, their behaviour also has to change, and sometimes quite radically. In my experience facilitating insight has to go hand in hand with cognitive and behavioural interventions made at the right time.

At first it can be very difficult to know which self is present in a session. It takes time to get really attuned: to get names, ages, the reason for that self developing, some history, their coping mechanisms and their reason for being there now. As time goes on it is easier to recognize the selves, because they look and sound different. They can apparently change physically, so that child selves can actually seem smaller. Voices change, gestures change, and different selves dress differently with their own styles of presenting themselves. When working with multiple personality clients I recognize more and more of the selves more and more easily as time goes on, but there usually remain selves I do not recognize.

Another therapeutic issue is that different selves have different needs, which makes for hard work for the client and for the therapist. It is easy to overlook this, especially if there is a controlling self preventing other selves from speaking. Transference with a multiple personality client is not simply from one individual to another: a group of selves is involved and can therefore produce a variety of transferential responses. Similarly, in my case my counter-transference is complicated, coming from a group of selves who can respond differently to the material. One example of these different transference responses is when I returned after an absence caused by ill health, and one client with multiple personality withdrew into an angry silence that took many weeks to break. She finally expressed rage by shouting, 'I trusted you, you betrayed me, you're just like my father, you let me down.' A different self said. 'I thought I had killed you,' while another said, 'I love you and I thought you were going to die.' At that time, while I knew this client has many different selves, I did not know which self was feeling and saying what. It took many months to find this out.

I have indicated that the behaviour of some selves ultimately has to be challenged and changed, and the question of challenge and confrontation is important. Behaviour patterns need to be confronted appropriately. Behavioural patterns, ideas and feelings are often initially unconscious, and the counsellor needs to begin to bring these into the client's conscious awareness so they can be acknowledged and worked with. This is not straightforward in multiple personality, as so many different behaviour patterns emerge. It is this very complexity that perhaps leads to medication rather than exploration and confrontation. The counselling process believes in tussling with these complexities, as opposed to medication, which believes in suppressing symptoms, thus avoiding the face-to-face struggle with another human being. It takes time to explore issues – perhaps to some it seems cheaper and easier to medicate.

As a counsellor working with women with multiple personality I recognize how painful the process is, but I nevertheless have expectations of each woman I see. They have already suffered too much from the devaluing effects of lack of expectations and from being treated as worthless. Throughout childhood many have often been called 'stupid', including me. When I went into adult education and realized I had difficulties I was given time and help, and I became a grade A student. I felt valued, believed in, and that there were expectations of me. I thrived on this. Likewise clients can thrive. For example, one woman with multiple personality was able to start her own business; others have returned to education and become counsellors themselves. I expect women in counselling to work with their side of the contract, in the same way as I work with mine – it is a two way process.

In my approach I emphasize a clear counselling contract, including the formalizing of therapeutic goals and the monitoring of them. Contracts are initially for 12 weeks, renewable on a six-weekly basis. With women with multiple personality this can create difficulties and the contract may be reviewed more often. There may be selves who do not understand the counselling process or the contract (for example, young selves may not understand such language); others may not be taking part and some may not want to know about me. When other selves decide to join in the counselling a new contract is needed. There can be selves who test me out and others who may need things from the relationship that would not normally be part of coun-selling: a walk in the park, shopping, a prison visit. Other selves may be wary of these things. This needs to be explored. Wariness of these aspects of the therapy is often because the client does not trust my preparedness to do something different, and feels that she should not need this from me.

One of my responsibilities is to find different ways of communicating with all the selves. This can include painting, drawing, writing, using work books, Dictaphones and keeping journals. These ways of working can be immensely helpful, but should never be used collusively to avoid feelings. Essentially I am prepared to offer a range of different therapeutic styles for different selves – as other therapists do for different types of client: if working with adolescents, for instance, a counsellor expects to work differently than if working with a child or an adult. I work in contexts other than the coun-selling room; but if, for example, I go to the park and play with clients, this is part of a therapeutic plan, not merely a whim. I learn more from an hour spent in this way than I do in hours spent counselling over many months. If I adopt a more flexible and extended model the different selves are able to reveal themselves more easily and naturally. In one sense I have adopted in individual work a model more usually seen in a therapeutic community. I can see that a team model might be helpful, with different workers involved. I also draw upon a crisis intervention model and see a client very promptly in an emergency, since this is an important point to intervene. This emphasizes my belief that to work with this presentation the model needs to be creative and flexible. A normal counselling/therapy framework may not be sufficient or appropriate. I emphasize that this is not boundary breaking, but having a different concept of boundaries.

Trust is very fragile for those who have been abused and especially so with multiple personality, since issues of trust are present for all the selves, if manifested in different ways. If trust is not worked with sufficiently – and in my experience it often is not – this can be a major barrier. Similarly, issues of power can be insufficiently worked with. Those who have been abused have experienced the absolute control of others, and tend to feel either in or out of control. There is no experience of negotiation in relationships. They can feel that allowing dependency on another gives that person control over them. Trust develops through the counsellor's consistency and reliability, but with multiple personality consistency is complex: it has to be addressed with each new self, bearing in mind their developmental level. Developing trust with one self does not automatically lead to trust by another self. There may be a destructive personality who wants to sabotage the trust being developed with the other selves. Younger selves can be influenced by older selves who feel that trusting anyone is dangerous.

This is further complicated by some selves not trusting one another. They continue to keep secrets for fear of not being believed by the others. They withdraw and do not wish to share their experiences. There is often a self who questions the validity of the experiences, in just the way often seen in the wider society. It is a difficult task for the counsellor, as one mistake or misunderstanding can trigger all the earlier mistrust. The counsellor has to remember how vulnerable each personality is. This has to be kept constantly on the agenda. My aim is to create a 'good enough' relationship with all the selves.

Boundaries of all sorts are generally recognized as crucial to maintaining the safety of counselling for client and counsellor. In multiple personality the creation and maintenance of boundaries is crucial. One question that arises is whether or not physical touch breaks boundaries or is an effective part of the healing process. This is particularly pertinent where child personalities may have a desperate need for comforting touch. Bennett and Braun state: 'Touch is an essential and potent therapeutic tool and as such must be treated with respect' (1986: 23).

Others argue that touch is rarely helpful or appropriate:

It is not necessarily helpful to alleviate pain prematurely. A second reason for not touching is that such a movement towards a client can easily be taken as threatening. A third reason for avoiding touch is that to some clients it may appear to encourage attachment to the counsellor.

(Jacobs 1988: 138)

Another view is expressed by Bass and Davies (1988: 351): 'Sometimes that hug is the very first time in that woman's life that she has been able to receive a nurturing touch, free of sexuality. Many of the women I work with are starved of safe touch.'

The line between safe touch and abusive touch may be hard to draw, but as the relationship develops and we have talked and explored with all the selves their feelings about touch, I allow a client to hug me and I hug them. But with multiple personality there can be selves within the system who dislike or fear touch and will not tolerate it, and this too has to be respected.

Another key boundary question relates to the counsellor revealing information about herself. There are times when I share my own experiences with the client. This helps to diminish their experience of being judged by another person, helps to equalize the power balance and prevents the client becoming too fearful. I have learnt from my own experience as a client: the first time I was in therapy the therapist sat in silence. I did not recognize this as an aspect of a particular therapeutic style. I was fearful; I did not like her silence; I did not like the way she sat there. Her silence took me back to childhood, and the fear that something bad was going to happen. I explore with a client why they need to know about me, but honesty on my part is vital from the beginning of the relationship. Of course, sharing personal life experiences can also hinder the process. It can help the client avoid issues, and can make the client feel resentful, angry and powerless.

In all my counselling work with women I am intensely aware of issues of power. This is particularly true when working with multiple personality, where women have so often experienced the ongoing impact of the power of others continually used against them. Women often describe themselves as never having had any power, because it was taken away by perpetrators, by the medical profession and by societal attitudes towards women. Counsellors can also exploit their position too easily so that clients who have experienced persecution can find this repeated in therapy. Counsellors and therapists need to work to help women discover the power in themselves. Perry writes (1993: 91): 'Women need to own the "male" parts of themselves. By this I mean characteristics such as single mindedness, the ability to compartmentalize, to be able to take ultimate responsibility, to act powerfully.'

The power of women can increase in counselling through the therapeutic relationship only when female counsellors are aware of such issues and can 'own the male parts of themselves' and thereby help clients to do the same. Women are still not encouraged to acknowledge or explore their power. Price writes that 'both men and women are frightened of the connection between aggression and sexuality' (1994: 269). This fear leads to avoidance of power issues, which is particularly difficult for survivors of abuse where aggression and sex have been inextricably intertwined. The counsellor must be aware of the stereotyping and collusion that reinforces women's powerlessness and thereby invalidates them.

Awareness of power is crucial in work with multiple personality, as another layer is involved – that of power issues between the different selves. These have to be addressed since the personalities have to learn to compromise so that ultimately they can work in harmony together. Personalities can also be abusive to one another, reflecting much of the abuse experienced throughout their lives. My aim is to give each personality a different message to internalize, which will enable the selves to care for each other rather than to be abusive.

Language is a powerful medium, and as a counsellor working with multiple personality I am particularly aware of how I use it. I am very careful not to put words into a client's mouth and do not use words like 'abuse' unless this reflects the vocabulary already used. I take great care never to be suggestive. The language used by society, by clients and by counsellors can be destructive. I encourage clients and supervisees to explore words and phrases. Jargon can be frightening, patronizing and hurtful, making clients feel powerless and unsafe and preventing them from owning and exploring their own experience. There are particular issues of working in a multi-cultural context, where a client's first language may not even include the vocabulary to describe abuse and where using a second language is inevitably more difficult. Because of my own experience of multiple personality I am aware that the perceptions of language can be very different according to the ages of selves. The style of language used by the different selves in therapy can help the therapist to identify who is present and can also indicate whether this is a baby, child, teenager, grown up or original self.

Working with Liza

On reading Liza's story I respect her understanding of herself as being multiple personality, but there are areas I want to check out. As a starting point for counselling I want to know more about the effects of all her experiences on her daily life. I want to know more about the dissociation: multiple personality is an ongoing process of dissociation at a deep level, where the splits take on a life of their own. There is certainly evidence in Liza's account that this is what has happened. I would encourage her to ask questions of me; I want it to be a very open process with the questions around multiplicity can be clearly stated. I will normalize the multiplicity, in terms of this being a valid experience for her that can be talked about, looked at, explored and discussed. I will encourage Liza to share her fantasies relating to multiple personality. Right from the beginning I want to avoid secrets.

Initially I will check out what brings her to therapy now; and whether there are any particular triggers. I will talk with the selves who are initially present and set up a contract with them. I want to identify and explore their aims. The contract provides a safe framework and boundaries for Liza – very important in terms of the lack of safety and invasion of boundaries in her history. The aims are to be flexible and fluid; they will inevitably change and develop as time goes on and more selves emerge.

Working on the dissociation will be crucial in my work with Liza, but working on both this and switching between personalities cannot begin before I know the different selves. I return to this later. My initial aim with Liza is to get to know them, by talking to each different self, getting to know their ways, and gathering information which will help both myself and Liza. Information about the selves includes name, if any; the age the self was when created; and the reason the personality developed. It is like trying to construct a three dimensional jigsaw, each piece consisting of different memories, different personalities, ages and ways of being. I aim to help Liza's different selves to get to know one another and to talk together. This takes time, perhaps even a year's work just to begin this process. Sometimes I will not know which self is present but I will ask Liza if she can tell me – it can be talked about. Sometimes she may not know or may not want to tell me.

This process of Liza's selves beginning to know one another is crucial. At first some may not like one another: one self can be suspicious of another, wondering what she knows. There can be powerful disagreements and arguments between them. It is a lot for the counsellor to hold, and a very good memory is needed. I will need to remember all the personalities and their memories and experiences, but also who likes whom, what they think of the others, and who is in touch with whom. There may be a facilitator or 'information self' present who helps in this process, sometimes telling the counsellor what other personalities need –for example, the young ones who may not be able to speak for themselves. Work with Liza will be facilitated by her being some way along in the process: she is coming to counselling already knowing what is troubling her, recognizing it and able to speak about it.

As the work progresses and I begin to know and relate to Liza's different selves, I will become increasingly aware of the extent to which she dissociates and I will work to help her to become more consciously aware of this. I expect dissociation and switching to occur in sessions and it will be crucial to work with this when the time is right and when Liza was ready. This will be at a later stage in the therapy; worked with too early it can silence the selves. I will then work with her to go through and explore the events and memories that she needs to dissociate. I will begin to help her to identify the triggers to this, both in our sessions and in her past. Once the triggers have been identified cognitive and grounding techniques can help people control dissociating. I have to be very sensitive and very aware in counselling sessions to note the points when she switches from one personality to another. Experience tells me that I am good at doing this – partly through having come to recognize the same process in myself. I can see and feel when this is happening, although of course for Liza it is a deeply unconscious process.

I look for signs in the expression of the eyes and the face. These are difficult to describe precisely, although they are visually very evident: a sense of deadness, of absence and of distance. It looks and feels as if something has gone; something that should be there is not – a feeling that the essential life of the person has gone. I therefore aim at making the unconscious conscious; recognizing that this has to be a slow and gentle process, and that deep defences are beginning to be dismantled.

I will also work with her to help her to recognize when and why she switches from one personality to another. I will work with her own experiences of this as she brings them to sessions – for example, I will help her to work through what happened to her in the shop. If in time I can help Liza to stop switching in a session then this will help her to begin to have some control over this in the rest of her life. Dissociation can be difficult to deal with it in itself, but switching from being in one self to another is different. It is a deeper layer to dissociation. It may have been life saving to the child Liza, but can be very unhelpful to the adult. From her own account we see that it can be deeply confusing, getting in the way of her leading her life as she would like to. My understanding is that Liza learned to dissociate in childhood as a result of the abuse she suffered, and that through the force of appalling circumstance, clear splits and distinct personalities were formed. In my view the development of multiple personality in Liza comes from events that have been so traumatic that her only way to survive has been to create separate worlds and personalities.

My role as the counsellor is to help Liza to work through her feelings, thoughts and emotions and to support her through the reliving of traumatic experiences. Together Liza and I need to identify the traumatic events experienced by the different selves and work through these experiences with all of them. This can be a terrifying and overwhelming experience for the client and can require a considerable input of time from the counsellor. Extra time may be needed when traumas are encountered, and this can also be the case when little ones or teenagers are present in the session. If this occurs with Liza, and I expect it to be part of the pattern of working with her, then I am aware that a 50-minute session sitting in a room will not be sufficient. If I am to work with longer sessions with Liza, I make this clear at the beginning of the session – I do not just let it happen. It might be a *different* time frame but there is still a frame, and I always bring the session to the end at the specified time. If Liza is particularly distressed I will make it clear that at those times she can have access to me between sessions. Some may argue that this is open to abuse but in my experience this need not be the case.

Because of the potential need for extra time I will only take Liza on if I am sure that I have sufficient resources available. This work can be a huge demand on time and if it becomes necessary I am prepared to see Liza five times a week. Although I cannot know if that level of support will be needed, I feel very strongly that it must be made available as long as I am sure I can maintain this. This level of contact can be required at times of real crisis, particularly when considerable material relating to the abuse is resurfacing. This is often when the client ends up in hospital or on heavy medication, unless more time is given. It is clear from Liza's story that hospitalization is neither what she wants nor what she needs and may result in experiences becoming buried rather than being looked at and explored. In addition, it is of course exceedingly expensive. One of my aims with Liza is to work to prevent hospital admission as this will not be therapeutic for her.

Extra time may also be needed when Liza's personalities are getting to know one another, when memories and events that have been kept separate start to come together. This can be terrifying and shocking. It is important for Liza and myself to explore other avenues of support, and ways of coping with daily life. Painful feelings are likely to intensify due to therapy. It can help, for example, to use survivor help lines or to keep and use a journal to record experiences and feelings. I want to look at what support she might have available from friends or partner. Support groups can also help, although these are difficult to find. I have in my work used other agencies when the need has arisen, for example, for help with children. Support is vital while in therapy and it needs to come from other sources than just the therapist. It can be arrogant and grandiose for counsellors to assume that by themselves they are always sufficient.

In sessions with Liza I want to give each self space. Like others with multiple personality Liza is likely to spend much energy controlling the selves to prevent others noticing. This can make her daily life particularly complicated. In counselling Liza I am trying to do the opposite – encouraging the selves to be there, to take space and to begin to meet their needs. It is important to give each person the same amount of time to avoid competition and envy arising – the familiar sibling cry of 'she's getting more than me – it's not fair' can also arise in work with multiple personality.

With Liza I expect there to be some selves who do not speak at all. It may be their role to be silent; they may not have the language and need to learn this in therapy; or they may be too tiny to speak. Part of my therapeutic role as I come to know Liza's child selves better is to provide them with some of the things they need, while always recognizing that I can never replace all that is lost. So for example I might go to the park with Liza if a child self needs this. I always carefully explore this first, in terms of its benefit and purpose. Such action needs to be part of a carefully considered therapeutic plan, not just because it vaguely seems a good idea. With clients with multiple personality I always work with a toy box, and I will talk with Liza about putting this together and what she would like in it, again being clear as to its purpose. This is to help the different selves to communicate with each other, to learn to play and to help the pre-verbal selves speak. The toys can be used symbolically by clients; for example, one used marbles to represent significant people in her life, providing a safe means for her to talk with them. Choosing items for the toy box can be complicated: at the shops a little self might want something and an adult self might challenge this or not allow this. So my role is to encourage their choices; to allow them both their voice and their needs. It is important to help the person overcome their embarrassment at wanting these things: they are used to being misunderstood and not having rights. Essentially I am concerned to help Liza discover other ways of talking. Other forms of therapy may include shopping, watching videos, drawing and painting, going for a walk or having a picnic. Drawing the different selves and seeing what they look like, as well as just hearing them, might help Liza get to know them.

I will work with Liza on a mapping system aimed at helping her to recover her memories. This shows all the personalities, developing as the therapy develops and including all the information relating to the different personalities as they emerge: their ages, their ways of being, the abuse that took place, and what they are like. I will use this to help Liza build a complete picture of each person's life. It becomes a systematic and ongoing record that can be referred to and worked with. It can include details from marriage and birth certificates and from doctors' reports. All this can be a valuable source of information for the survivor, and if Liza has not accessed these I might suggest that she does. Essentially we try to build up a picture of Liza's world, which in sessions can help Liza and myself locate which personality is present. We can also use it to help the personalities to know one another as a step towards helping them to live in harmony. The more information Liza has, and the more aware she becomes, the more control she will have over her life.

I might also use a journal with Liza; I will discuss this with her when she first comes. Some people find this helpful, others do not. I will talk with her to see if she is prepared to do this. As each self emerges I invite them to keep a journal, so Liza could have several. They can write between sessions and bring the journals to sessions if they want to. This may not be straightforward. If Liza has a 'facilitator self', that self may bring the journal, but the self who has written it may not always come out. In that event it is not possible to use it: I have to wait until that person is ready to share. I will make it clear to Liza that I do not keep secrets, so what the selves say is but only to be shared when the moment is right. Otherwise there can be collusion, like so much that has happened in her abusive family. Careful timing is crucial. I hold information – as therapists always do – until it is appropriate to put it back into the work. If I move into difficult areas too quickly I might silence some of Liza's personalities.

I expect issues relating to boundaries, trust and power to be threads that will run throughout the work with Liza; and these will always have a place on our agenda – they will be part of the process throughout. With her history of abuse inevitably issues of power and trust will be there for all of Liza's personalities to a greater or lesser degree and might take many forms. It is therefore essential that each of her different selves takes the time they need to get to know me, and for me to recognize that some will take longer than others. With Liza I will work with the issue of boundaries with each self as it emerges. Reading her story I think that some selves will push hard at boundaries and others will not.

The question is often asked about how long a client with multiple personality needs in counselling, and whether all the personalities have to be involved. I cannot give a clear answer as this can vary tremendously. It is possible for only one autonomous self, who has their own feelings, thoughts, emotions and life experience, to enter counselling or therapy and for this sort of client to use shorter-term counselling. Another pattern is for one self to enter therapy while the rest observe. This is a very different scenario; in the first, only one self is present and there are no observers present. Other clients with multiple personality clearly need long-term therapy since it takes time for selves to emerge, and it takes time to recognize and work with different ways of communicating. Some personalities initially have no language base with which to share their memories. If these factors are present time is essential: this is not work that can be rushed. Deep defences are involved and these must be respected.

Overall, my aim is to help Liza to recognize and live with her different selves so that they are working harmoniously and are not in conflict with one another. I want to help her to work through the traumas that she has had to split off so that she begins to feel in control of these, and so they do not continually interfere with her life. I want to work with her to become aware of the dissociating, to recognize the triggers, and ultimately to be able to live with her experiences comfortably enough that she does not need to disappear in this way. I want to help her to find other ways of coping that are more constructive, and enable her to feel part of the world in the way she wants.

Particular issues for counsellors and therapists with multiple personalities

I do not believe that counsellors have to have experienced abuse, or to be multiple personality, to work in this area. When I first entered therapy I felt that the therapist could not possibly understand. But ten years on this view has changed. What is crucial is the ability to live in someone else's world without mistaking it for your own. Before I could work with multiple personality I had to accept it and understand it in myself. While I was beginning to identify in my own therapy that I had multiple personalities I was working with people who had been abused, but I could not have worked with people with multiple personality. Counsellors with multiple personality need to have worked through their own issues sufficiently so that their different selves are working in harmony. Otherwise a re-enactment can occur, with the counsellor reliving her own experiences. She may become another person who is abusive to the client. The counsellor might then defend herself by avoiding or denying; or she might become traumatized. Splitting on the counsellor's part might result, although this possibility exists in all therapeutic situations where the therapist's unresolved issues are triggered by a client.

There can be issues for both counsellor and client when they are both multiple personality. For instance, Liza might worry that her material will distress me and cause another of my personalities to come in and take over. This is a possibility and it would be false to assure her absolutely that this will not happen. But I know that when my different selves are working in harmony, this will not arise and if they were not in harmony I would not work with multiple personality. The way I work is based on negotiation. I am open with clients and I can envisage saying to Liza, if our relationship becomes good enough, that a particular week may not be for me the right time to explore a particular area. Supervision is crucial to help me monitor how I am and where I am.

There are advantages to being multiple personality myself: for example with Liza I might be more aware of the switching between personalities. While it is important not to jump to conclusions, I am very able to recognize the signs of switching, and have a very acute awareness of what may have triggered this. My own experience gives me a valuable edge in recognizing what may be happening to Liza. I am very able to stay with the muddle of multiple personality which Liza describes vividly. I am comfortable in staying with the chaos: after all I have help, and I know well what it is like to be in the midst of it.

I have a very special insight into what it is like to have multiple personality. This understanding gives me the strength and the ability to grasp easily in therapy what others may have more difficulty in understanding. There can of course be problems, depending on where therapists are in their own life and adjustment. Therapy has been crucial for me in ensuring that all my personalities are likely to be working together towards an agreed purpose and a common goal. As a counsellor who has been abused and who has multiple personality I need to be careful not to mistake the client's world for my own. It is vital that I do not make assumptions: how it was for me is not the same as how it is for the client. However, I come from a different starting point because of my experience, and although this has to be monitored to ensure that negative effects do not result, it can positively assist the process.

Conclusion

In working with multiple personality one has to recognize that it is not like other counselling. For example, there is not always a neat 50-minute session. It will not work: a traditional structure is not sufficient. The counsellor or therapist needs to recognize that they are gathering not just one history but the history of a group of people. At first it seems an enormous task to make sense of where the different histories might fit in. The therapist then has to work with each self, to deal with the experiences and memories they are holding. I myself query the concept of integration, and see living in harmony as a more helpful view. To do this all the selves must have a chance to speak and to be heard. Conflicts have to be reduced and managed, and compromises made between selves. The therapist is validating the existence and experiences of each self, but also beginning to help them to behave responsibly. This may mean helping the person to say 'no' to some of them.

Boundaries have to be held very carefully, but they are in a different context. This needs to be understood since to those working in other contexts some of what goes on in this work might seem to be boundary breaking. This is not so, but rather a creative move into another framework. Perhaps therapist creativity and clear boundaries do not often go hand in hand. The framework is in contrast with the traditional: sessions can be more frequent, longer, child personalities may play, be taken to the park or bought presents. This is a different therapeutic language. What is central is that these aspects are always talked about as part of the process. These aspects are not just acted upon, but are thought out, talked through and worked with. There is never any excuse for an inappropriate breaking of therapeutic boundaries although I have seen that happen. To work with multiple personality a counsellor must be very containing and very clear on boundaries, and yet at the same time able to take an imaginative leap. Therapists and counsellors need to be creative in a world that is difficult to understand and conceptualize, and where the structure of the person has a different base. This may be too threatening to people who like clarity and an absolute base to work from.

References

Bass, E. and Davies, L. (1988) *The Courage to Heal*. New York: Harper and Row.

Bennett, G. and Braun, M. D. (1986) *Treatment of Multiple Personality Disorder*. American Psychiatric Press.

Bloom, S. (1994) Creating sanctuary: ritual abuse and complex post-traumatic stress disorder, in V. Sinason (ed.) *Treating Survivors of Satanist Abuse*. London: Routledge.

Freud, S. (1991) *The Aetiology of Hysteria. New Introductory Lectures in Psychoanalysis*. London: Penguin. (First published 1896.)

Jacobs, M. (1988) *Psychodynamic Counselling in Action*. London: Sage.

Perry, J. (1993) *Counselling for Women*. Buckingham: Open University Press.

Price, J. (1988) Single-sex therapy groups, in M. Aveline and W. Dryden (eds) *Group Therapy in Britain*. Buckingham: Open University Press.

Summit, R. C. (1988) Hidden victims, hidden pain, in G. E. Wyatt and G. J. Powell (eds) *Lasting Effects of Child Sexual Abuse*. London: Sage.

Walker, M. (1993) *Surviving Secrets*. Buckingham: Open University Press.

Wyatt, G. E. and Powell, G. J. (1988) Later psychological problems, in G. E. Wyatt and G. J. Powell (eds) *Lasting Effects of Child Sexual Abuse*. London: Sage.

Chapter 8

Hidden selves: a summary

Moira Walker

In this book readers have been presented with the story of one survivor, who identifies herself as having many personalities, followed by the responses of six clinicians to this account. These responses cover a range of carefully considered but diametrically opposed views, although they have in common a deep concern for Liza that is actively communicated in all the chapters. Both Peter Dale and Graz Kowszun write from a sceptical standpoint. They clearly respect Liza's views and perceptions of her self, but want to challenge and question her self-diagnosis of having multiple personalities, querying both the source of her belief in her multiplicity and the validity of the concept. Dale wonders if Liza might make better progress therapeutically if she were free of this 'belief system', and he explores and examines other explanations for her experiences. He expresses concern that her initial awareness of multiplicity was triggered by reading a book, and wonders about how suggestible she might be. While recognizing that most therapeutic interventions are unlikely to be as suggestible and forceful as they are at the extreme end of the spectrum described in some literature from the United States, he does wonder about more subtle therapeutic influencing.

Kowszun is similarly sceptical, and takes up the issue of fashions in therapy. She focuses on a social constructionist approach as explaining both Liza's presentation and self-understanding, and the concept of multiple personality in general. She reminds us of the wide spectrum of language, ideas and concepts that already variously exist in our therapeutic vocabulary and in our attempts to define, understand and describe structures of the self and the mind. For her these are already extensive and sufficient, and the addition of multiple personality is both unnecessary, and potentially unhelpful and inaccurate. Like Dale, she expresses concern over the numbers of people being diagnosed as multiple in the United States. She suggests that this raises significant and important questions about the validity of the diagnosis and that it also emphasizes her point about diagnostic fashions.

Jenifer Antony-Black is coming from the very particular standpoint of being multiple herself, and she describes in her chapter how her own experiences are essentially interwoven with her therapeutic stance. Although she is absolute in her conviction of the existence of multiple personality as a creative response to extreme abuse, nevertheless she does share with Dale a concern over assisting Liza to cope with the impact on her everyday life, and agrees that cognitive-behavioural interventions have an important role to play. However, she sees this as only one aspect of the work and her therapeutic role – one that in itself would be insufficient.

John and Marcia Davis are similarly convinced that multiple personality exists, understanding this from a traumatogenic standpoint. They describe, as do other practitioners who have encountered this presentation, how multiple personality came to them: they were not searching for it. This is in direct contradiction to some of the literature I describe in Chapter 1, with its theme of therapist as detective searching for multiplicity. They examine in some detail the process of dissociation and splitting, noting that as yet there is much we do not understand. Like Antony-Black, they provide the reader with a detailed and fascinating account of how they might work with Liza.

Phil Mollon provides the reader with another example of how an experienced practitioner began to recognize multiple personality in the course of everyday clinical work. He again was not looking for it, nor was he trained to recognize it. It was rather clinical presentations which informed his thinking and suggested that his existing knowledge and awareness were insufficient for what he was encountering. Unlike many practitioners and writers from the United States, Mollon's experience suggests that multiple personality is a relatively rare occurrence, although the Davises would argue differently. Mollon also describes how in his training dissociation and its possible causes was given scant attention. He reminds the reader of how recently abuse and dissociation went unstudied and unrecognized in psychotherapy training. Psychotherapists simply did not work with abuse. This is perhaps, a timely reminder of the fact that if something is not recognized it cannot by definition be known to exist.

Readers will decide for themselves how they would understand and respond personally and therapeutically to Liza's story. I am amazed yet again in reading her account of how much the child and the adult can survive, and of how psychological manoeuvrings can underpin such survival. Doubtless all those involved with this book, whether as editors, authors or readers, will have been moved by her account of her life, and the horrors of the abuse she suffered both as a child and as an adult. All those who are working with clients like Liza will be forcibly struck by the huge responsibility of the therapist, counsellor, or other helper in being with someone who has already suffered so considerably. The greatest care is needed and the highest standards must continually be their aim.

In Chapter 1 I make clear the stage that my own thinking on multiple personality has reached. It has been enthralling to work on this book, both with therapists who share my views and with therapists who do not. Hopefully it is the bringing together of disparate thinking in this way that can enliven debate, spotlight key questions and ensure that none of us – whatever views we hold – becomes complacent or over-confident. The book reinforces what we have already learnt in beginning to face the extent and consequences of abuse, and in struggling to overcome denial: there is always so much that we do not know. There are always problematic challenges to be made and uncomfortable questions to be put. The ability to face our own assumptions and resistances gradually extends the scope and nature of our learning. It is Jenifer Antony-Black's hope and mine, as editors, that this book has played a part in the ongoing process of discovery, challenge and knowledge.

SURVIVING SECRETS
THE EXPERIENCE OF ABUSE FOR THE CHILD, THE ADULT AND THE HELPER

Moira Walker

In recent years considerable attention has been paid to the subject of abuse in childhood. Less attention has been paid to what happens to the vast number of women and men who have reached adulthood with this experience haunting them. Moira Walker overviews the experience and its implications, dealing with physical, sexual and psychological abuse. An essential part of the content is based on interviews with survivors of child abuse, voicing their views on the effects of the experience and the effectiveness of the help offered. At the same time, *Surviving Secrets* seeks to understand the context in which abuse takes place, the society which itself contains and sustains abuse at various levels. It is a moving account of the experience and effects of childhood abuse, and a hand-book for all those in the caring professions, in voluntary organizations and else-where who are helping survivors of abuse.

Contents
Introduction – A web of secrets: generations of abuse – Adults reflect: the child's experi-ence – Childhood abuse: the adult's experience – Sharing secrets: the child's and the adult's experience – The development of Multiple Personality Disorder – Stages in the process of counselling and therapy – Particular issues in the process of therapy – Issues for the helper – References – Index.

224pp   0 335 09763 4 (Paperback)   0 335 09764 2 (Hardback)

PETA – A FEMINIST'S PROBLEM WITH MEN

Moira Walker (ed.)

'I've got a problem with men . . . I don't know whether it's a problem with other things as well . . . I am afraid of what men represent . . . I feel they have more power.'

This is how Peta begins to tell her story to her potential therapist. Six therapists are given the opportunity of assessing Peta: What do they wish to know about her? How do they understand her? How might they work with her? And what outcome can they predict for her as a result of therapy?

In this fascinating book – which starts with Peta's own story – the reader has the chance to see six different therapists at work, drawing on the same initial material from the one real client. The similarities and differences between therapies and therapists are highlighted. And at the end the reader is able to enter Peta's experience of the process, and decide with her, which one she might choose in her search for a therapist.

This highly original volume will appeal to a wide range of students and practitioners involved in counselling and psychotherapy, particularly those interested in comparing different therapeutic approaches.

Contents
The editors: in search of the client – Peta: a feminist's problem with men – The reader's response – Jennifer Mackewn: Gestalt psychotherapy – Judy Moore: person-centred psychotherapy – John Ormrod: cognitive behaviour therapy – John Rowan: humanistic and integrative psychotherapy – Maye Taylor: feminist psychotherapy – Christine Wood: art therapy – Moira Walker and Peta: review and response.

Contributors
Jennifer Mackewn, Judy Moore, John Ormrod, John Rowan, Maye Taylor, Christine Wood.

168pp   0 335 19223 8 (Paperback)

MORAG – MYSELF OR MOTHER HEN?

Moira Walker (ed.)

I don't like cleaning and hoovering and washing up. I do them because I have to, and I feel that James wants me to be in the house, to be there because his children are there, and the family's there . . . he likes me there being the mother-hen!

This is how Morag begins to tell her story to her potential therapist. Six therapists are given the opportunity of assessing Morag: What do they wish to know about her? How might they work with her? And what outcome can they predict for her as a result of therapy?

In this highly original book – which start with Morag's own story – the reader has a chance to see six different therapists at work, drawing on the same material from the one real client. The similarities and differences between therapies are highlighted. And at the end the reader is able to enter Morag's experience of the process, and decide with her, which one she might choose in her search for a therapist.

This fascinating volume will appeal to a wide range of students and practitioners involved in counselling and psychotherapy, particularly those interested in comparing different therapeutic approaches.

Contents
The editors: in search of the client – Morag: myself or mother hen? – The reader's response – Roxanne Agnew: focused expressive psychotherapy – Windy Dryden: rational emotive behaviour therapy – Paul Holmes: psychodrama – Arthur Jonathan: existential psychotherapy – Anthea Millar: Adlerian therapy – Peter Savage: hypnotherapy – Moira Walker and Morag: review and response.

Contributors
Roxanne Agnew, Windy Dryden, Paul Holmes, Arthur Jonathan, Anthea Millar, Peter Savage.

176pp   0 335 19224 6 (Paperback)

WOMEN IN THERAPY AND COUNSELLING
OUT OF THE SHADOWS

Moira Walker

Moira Walker asserts that women live in a society that exerts powerful pressures upon them. She argues that when women present for counselling it is essential to understand and acknowledge the interactions between their inner and outer worlds. In this way political, societal and historical frameworks, as well as individual dynamics, must be appreciated if women's difficulties are not to be trivialized. The use of clinical material not only demonstrates the value of such an approach, but also provides a framework in which to describe the counselling process. Those who work with women will find valuable guidelines for appropriate interventions that take account of these complexities.

> Reading this book was an experience that was both heart-warming and enraging: heart-warming because of the wisdom and sensitivity of the author's treatment of her subject; enraging because it brings home not just the oppression and sheer difficulty of most women's lives, but also just how inappropriate much psychological theory, counselling and therapy have been and continue to be . . . She integrates social history, academic, psychological and feminist theory with hard reality in a highly readable way. Recommended: should be required for all who work with women.
>
> *Self and Society*

> While the book would make interesting reading for anyone wanting to understand women better, for those working with them it is essential.
>
> *Nursing Times*

> The 'story' is beautifully and compassionately told . . . The wealth of detail and the fascinating glimpses into the counsellor's own formulations and connections give the reader access to 'private worlds' in a manner which is neither patronising nor intrusive.
>
> *Counselling Psychology Review*

Contents

208pp   0 335 09375 2 (Paperback)   0 335 09376 0 (Hardback)